Study Guide to
The Sympathizer
by
Viet Thanh Nguyen

by Ray Moore

Contents

Preface

A study guide is an *aid* to the close reading of a text; it is *never* a substitute for reading the text itself. This novel deserves to be read *reflectively*, and the aim of this guide is to facilitate such a reading. The Guiding Questions have *no* answers provided. This is a deliberate choice. The questions are for readers who want to come to *their own conclusions* about the text and not simply to be told what to think about it by someone else. Even 'suggested' answers would limit the *exploration of the text* by readers themselves which is the primary aim of the guide.

In the classroom, I found that students frequently came up with answers that I had not even considered, and, not infrequently, that they expressed their ideas better than I could have done. The point of this guide is to *open up* the text, not to close it down by providing 'ready-made answers.' Teachers do not need their own set of predetermined answers in order effectively to evaluate the responses of their students.

In the Notes and Commentaries section, the notes briefly explain the most important names, words and phrases used by the author and the many historical and geographical references in the novel, and the commentaries analyze the most significant points of each chapter. The commentaries do not set out to answer the guiding questions, but sometimes they do cover the same ground. Each represents my best understanding of a chapter at this point in time. The commentaries make no claim to be complete and certainly not to be definitive. Feel free to disagree.

Acknowledgements

As always, I am indebted to the work of numerous reviewers and critics. Where I am conscious of having taken an idea or a phrase from a particular author, I have cited the source in the text. Any failure to do so is an omission which I will immediately correct if it is drawn to my attention.

I believe that all quotations used fall under the definition of 'fair use.' If I am in error on any quotation, I will immediately correct it.

Thanks are due to my wife, Barbara, for reading the manuscript, for offering valuable suggestions, and for putting the text into the correct formats for publication. Any errors which remain are my own.

Spoiler alert!

If you are reading the novel for the first time, you may wish to go straight to the Guiding Questions section and come back to the earlier sections later since they do explain everything that happens in the novel, including the ending!

Picture attribution

South Vietnamese refugees walk across a U.S. Navy vessel. Operation Frequent Wind, the final operation in Saigon, began April 29, 1975. During a nearly constant barrage of explosions, the Marines loaded American and Vietnamese civilians, who feared for their lives, onto helicopters that brought them to waiting aircraft carriers.

This photograph is in the public domain. Source: orlandoweekly.com

Introduction

Plot Summary

The unnamed narrator is a prisoner who is being forced to write his confessions by the Commandant of the prison. It is unclear where this prison is or what the narrator has done to get himself incarcerated, but these points are gradually clarified as the narrative develops. The narrator is the illegitimate son of a French priest and a poor Vietnamese peasant girl. Recruited in his youth to the communist cause by his close friend Man, he spent six years attending university in California, but returned to Vietnam, ostensibly to fight in defense of the anti-communist Republic of Vietnam but actually (like Man) to spy for the Viet Cong.

The narrator begins his story in April 1975 as the armed forces of North Vietnam are closing in on Saigon, the capital of South Vietnam. He is a captain and the trusted aide-de-camp of a Republican Vietnamese general who is the head of the police force in whose villa he lives with the General's wife and children. Of course, the General does not know that the captain is a communist agent assigned to spy on him. As it becomes clear that resistance to the communists is collapsing, the General secures from the CIA a flight out of the country, and his trusted captain makes a list of those who will be given places on one of the last flights out before Saigon falls and the communists take over.

The narrator's handler, Man, orders him to go to the USA and become a sleeper agent (i.e., a spy who goes undercover in a country for several years). The captain ensures that his other great friend Bon, a patriot who does not know that Man and the narrator are communists, can escape with his family on the same flight he is taking. However, during the evacuation, Bon's wife and young son are killed, leaving him deeply depressed.

Following some time in a resettlement camp in Guam, the captain begins a new life in Los Angeles with other members of the expatriot Vietnamese community. However, he is secretly observing and reporting on the General and other Vietnamese evacuees (including Bon) by writing secret messages in letters to his 'aunt' in Paris, from where they are passed on to Man who has stayed in Vietnam. The captain becomes a clerical assistant at the Department of Oriental Studies in a university, where he meets Sophia Mori, a middle-aged Japanese-American. Ms Mori and the captain, who share the experience of life as an Asian in America, have a sexual relationship, though the narrator becomes more emotionally involved than does Sophia.

The General begins to makes plans to return to Vietnam to fight the communists. He forms a front organization called the Fraternity as a conduit for funds to the military movement. He and his wife also open a restaurant to help with the funding, and he enlists the help of a Claude (a CIA operative whom he knew in Vietnam) and a Congressman to gather funds from various unofficial sources. When the General expresses to the captain his suspicion that there is a

3

spy in the organization, to throw the General's suspicion off himself, the captain names a fellow evacuee (a major) and, on the General's orders, he and his friend Bon shoot the man outside his house. The assassination is taken to be an armed robbery and it is never solved.

The narrator is asked by the General to review the script for a movie called *The Hamlet* which is about Green Berets in Vietnam. Initially, his criticisms of the way in which the film presents the Vietnamese people are rejected by the director, but he is then asked to go to the Philippines to ensure the accurate presentation of Vietnamese people in the shooting of the movie. His attempts to do this, however, lead to more conflict with the director. Near the conclusion of the shooting, he is injured in an explosion and eventually receives $10,000 in compensation. He feels that he has failed to make any significant change to the way the Vietnamese people are presented in the movie.

Back in California, he gives $5,000 to the major's widow; finds that his affair with Sophia is over (since she has begun an affair with his old acquaintance Sonny, a Vietnamese living in USA); and becomes involved in coordinating the General's plans to mount an invasion of Vietnam – plans which he shares with his Paris contact. Bon is determined to volunteer for what looks like a suicide mission because he wants to die; in order to try to save him, the captain decides (against the direct orders of Man) to return to Vietnam with him. At the General's 'suggestion' he shoots Sonny, a newspaper editor whose critical coverage of the military preparations of the Vietnam refugees has become embarrassing. Almost immediately after, the captain and his friend Bon fly to Thailand where they are met by Claude, the CIA operative. However, on their first armed patrol they are ambushed. Many members of the patrol are killed but Bon, the narrator and a few others are captured.

The sympathizer spends a year in solitary confinement writing draft after draft of his confession under the supervision of the prison Commandant. When this process is finished, he is passed onto the prison Commissar, who turns out to be Man – horribly disfigured in a napalm attack during the capture of Saigon. Man insists that his friend's confession is incomplete because he has still not admitted what he knows about the fate of a woman communist agent who was captured. Under 'enhanced interrogation' the sympathizer remembers that he was powerless to save the woman or to prevent her from being raped: he simply watched it happen.

Later in his reeducation, the captain admits (to himself probably for the first time) that he wrote to Man telling him that he wished his father were dead knowing that, in doing so, he was effectively ordering his father's murder. Man had the priest shot. Even this, however, is not enough. Finally, the sympathizer has to acknowledge that there is nothing "more precious than independence and freedom" (360). This satisfies the Commandant, since it seems to be a total acceptance of the communist ideology, in support of which nothing, however

4

cruel and inhuman, can be allowed to stand in its way. To the narrator and to Man, however, it means that nothing matters *more than* revolution. The revolution has failed to replace corruption and exploitation; it has merely changed the names of the corrupters and the exploiters.

Man arranges for the narrator and Bon to be released from prison, and through bribery he secures their escape from Saigon. They join the boat people desperate for a new start and having only the fact that they are alive to sustain them – but being alive is the whole point.

Why Read this Book

This debut novel won the 2016 Pulitzer Prize for Fiction and the Andrew Carnegie Medal for Excellence in Fiction and was named a Best Book of the Year by (among others) The New York Times Book Review, The Wall Street Journal, The Library Journal, and The Guardian.

The number of Americans who lived through the Vietnam War is inevitably shrinking. There are certainly still many thousands still alive who fought in Vietnam or knew someone who did. There are perhaps millions of Americans who followed the war as it unfolded in contemporary television and newspaper coverage. These, however, represent a small minority of the US population as a whole. The remainder has gathered such knowledge as they have from movies, documentaries, and history books. What *all* of these people (with the exception of members of the Vietnamese-American community) have in common is that, inevitably, they have viewed the Vietnam War from an American perspective which, as Nguyen has said, "totally excluded the Vietnamese experience" (Charlie Rose Interview). What this novel does is to provide the Vietnamese perspective (communist and anti-communist) on the war by tracing the experience of a group of characters through the final months of the rapid collapse of the South, the chaotic and bloody evacuation of Saigon, the resettlement process in Guam and California, and the planning of a renewed military intervention to destabilize the communist regime.

Issues with this Text

The author describes quite graphically the injuries and deaths of both civilians and military personnel sustained during in the conflict. There are also two detailed accounts of torture, including one in which a female communist agent is serially raped by her captors. I have known readers whose families were impacted by the Vietnam War to find the novel very disturbing.

The protagonist has several sexual encounters, though none is described in either a detailed or an erotic way. Occasionally, characters swear and blaspheme.

Although the narrative contains a great deal of direct speech, the author does not use speech marks to indicate direct speech. This can be a little confusing at first.

A Selective Timeline of the History of Vietnam

1802   The Nguyen Dynasty is founded and names the country Vietnam.

1858   France takes control of Vietnam which becomes a French colony.

1893   Vietnam becomes part of French Indochina which includes Tonkin, Annam, Cochin China, Laos and Cambodia.

1930   Ho Chi Minh, a communist trained in the U.S.S.R., founds the Indochinese Communist Party (I.C.P.).

1939   World War II begins.

1940   In September, Japanese troops invade French Indochina and take control of Vietnam. They encounter very little French resistance.

1941   In May, the I.C.P. establishes the League for the Independence of Vietnam, a guerrilla force, commonly called the Viet Minh, to resist Japanese occupying forces.

1945   World War II ends: France reoccupies Southern Vietnam and the Viet Minh seize control of North Vietnam. In September, Ho Chi Minh declares Vietnam an independent country. Ironically, he models his declaration on the American Declaration of Independence (1776) in an effort to win the support of the American government.

1946   In June, Ho Chi Minh rejects a French proposal offering Vietnam limited self-government, and the French-Viet Minh War begins. French forces attack the Viet Minh in Haiphong in November. The United States supports the French in an effort to prevent the spread of communism through Asia.

1947   In March, President Harry Truman tells Congress that the United States will assist any country threatened by communism. This comes to be called The Truman Doctrine.

1949   In June, the French install the former emperor Bao Dai as the Vietnamese head of state.

1950   In January, the Democratic Republic of Vietnam (the communist North) is officially recognized by China and U.S.S.R.

1954   Viet Minh forces attack the French military outpost in the town of Dien Bien Phu. The conflict

   lasts two months (March 13th to May 7th). Aware that it cannot win, the French government agrees to begin peace talks.

   In April, President Eisenhower says that the fall of French Indochina could create a 'domino-effect' in Southeast Asia (i.e., one country falls and then the next and then the next until the whole region is communist). The Domino Theory guides U.S. thinking on Vietnam for the next decade.

   In July, the Geneva Accords establish North and South Vietnam with the 17th parallel as the border. The agreement states that elections are to be held within two years to unify Vietnam under a single democratic government. The elections never take place.

1956   South Vietnamese President Ngo Dinh Diem initiates a crackdown against political dissidents. 1957Communist insurgents move into the South.

1959   The Vietnam War begins: Ho Chi Minh declares that it is the aim of the North to reunite Vietnam. Beginning in May, North Vietnam forces build a supply route through Laos and Cambodia to South Vietnam to provide fighters and material to support guerrilla attacks against Diem's government. This becomes known as the Ho Chi Minh Trail, and the Americans are never able to shut it down. In July, the first U.S. soldiers are killed in South Vietnam when guerillas attack their quarters near Saigon.

1960   The U.S.A. increases aid to President Diem. In December, the National Liberation Front (N.L.F.) is formed as the political wing of the insurgency in South Vietnam. The U.S. calls the N.L.F. the Viet Cong, which is short for Vietnam Cong-san (Vietnamese communists).

1961-2 The number of US 'advisors' rises to 12,000. They progressively take a more active role in military operations. In May 1961, President Kennedy sends helicopters and four hundred Green Berets to South Vietnam and authorizes secret operations against the Viet Cong. In January 1962, U.S. aircraft begin spraying Agent Orange and other herbicides over rural areas of South Vietnam to kill vegetation in order to deny cover and food to enemy forces.

1963   In January, South Vietnamese troops are defeated in the Mekong Delta by a much smaller number of Viet Cong fighters. Having faced increasing opposition, most notably from the Buddhist minority in the country, President Diem is overthrown and then killed in a military coup that has U.S. support. Between 1963 and 1965, there will be twelve further changes of government.

1964   The Gulf of Tonkin incident: the U.S. government *claims* that, on August 2nd, North Vietnamese patrol boats fired on two Navy destroyers. Congress approves the Gulf of Tonkin Resolution, authorizing military action in retaliation. (The 'attack' remains controversial. The weight of evidence suggests that it did not happen.) The U.S.S.R. and China increase military aid to the North.

1965   President Johnson launches Operation Rolling Thunder, a three-year bombing campaign (March 2nd, 1965 to November 1st, 1968) against North Vietnam and the Ho Chi Minh Trail. 200,000 American combat troops arrive in South Vietnam. From November 14th to 18th, almost 300 Americans are killed and hundreds injured in the Battle of la Drang Valley in the Central Highlands of South Vietnam.

1966   Total U.S. troop numbers 400,000.

1967   Total U.S. troop numbers 500,000. In April there are huge anti-war demonstrations across the U.S.A. In November, U.S. forces suffer 1,800 casualties in the Battle of Dak (November 3rd to 23rd) in the Central Highlands of the Republic of Vietnam.

1968   On January 30th , the North launches the Tet Offensive, a combined assault by Viet Cong and the North Vietnamese regular army forces on one hundred cities and outposts across South Vietnam, including Saigon, where the U.S. Embassy is overrun and temporarily occupied. In the week February 11th-17th, 543 American soldiers die. The Offensive ends on September 23rd. The communists are defeated, but at great cost (in 'blood and treasure') to the Americans. Allied casualties are: 4,124 killed, 19,295 wounded and 604 missing.

On March 16th, more than 500 civilians are massacred by U.S. forces at My Lai, causing increased revulsion against the war in America. On October 31st, President Johnson halts bombing in Vietnam north of the 20th parallel and states that he will "not seek and I will not accept the nomination of my party as your President."

1969   From March 1969 to May 1970, U.S. B-52 bombers target suspected communist base camps and supply zones in Cambodia. This operation is kept secret since Cambodia is officially a neutral country. In December, the U.S. institutes the first draft lottery since World War II. In the face of growing opposition to the war, President Nixon orders the reduction of U.S. ground troops in Vietnam. Ho Chi Minh, who has been ill for some time, dies.

1970   The U.S. national security advisor, Henry Kissinger, and Le Duc Tho, representing the Hanoi government, begin peace talks in Paris. From April to June, U.S. and South Vietnamese forces attack communist bases in Cambodia.

1971   From January to March, ARVN and US troops invade Laos in a costly and unsuccessful attempt to cut the Ho Chi Minh Trail. In June, *The New York Times* publishes leaked Defense Department (the Pentagon Papers) that detail the full extent of U.S. involvement in the war. Anti-war sentiment in the U.S.A. grows.

1972   In December, President Nixon orders intensive bombing of Hanoi and Haiphong (Operation Linebacker). 20,000 tons of bombs are dropped on densely populated regions in the most intense air offense of the war.

1973   On January 27th, the draft ends and President Nixon signs the Paris Peace Accords which stipulate that U.S. troops must withdraw by March.

1975   North Vietnamese forces invade South Vietnam and rapidly take control of the whole country as military resistance collapses. South Vietnamese President Duong Van Minh leaves the country (reportedly taking a great deal of gold with him). As Saigon is surrounded, the Americans desperately airlift 1,000 of their own personnel and 7,000 of those Vietnamese who have worked for them in an 18-hour evacuation effort. Many are left behind. The city of Saigon falls on Artil 30th and is renamed Ho Chi Minh City.

The war is over. More than 58,000 Americans, over one million North Vietnamese and Viet Cong, around 250,000 South Vietnamese soldiers, and more than two million civilians have died.

1976   The Socialist Republic of Vietnam is declared. Over the next decade or so, hundreds of thousands of refugees will flee abroad, many risking their lives in small boats in a desperate attempt to escape persecution.

1977   Vietnam is admitted to the United Nations.

1979   Vietnam invades Cambodia and ends the murderous Khmer Rouge regime of Pol Pot. In response, Chinese troops invade Vietnam's northern border but are pushed back by Vietnamese forces.

1986   More liberal economic policies, called Doi Moi, are introduced – an acknowledgement of the disastrous impact of communist reforms.

1989   Vietnamese troops withdraw from Cambodia.

1992   A new constitution is adopted allowing even greater economic freedoms although the Communist Party remains the sole authority in Vietnamese society.

1995   The United States and Vietnam establish full diplomatic relations.

2000   President Bill Clinton pays a four-day official visit to Vietnam (November 16th to 20th). The U.S. pledges more help to clear landmines left over from the war which are estimated to have killed almost 40,000 people.

2005   Prime Minister Phan Van Khai makes the first visit to the U.S. by a Vietnamese leader since the end of the Vietnam War.

2007   In February, the U.S. agrees to fund a study for the removal from a former base in Da Nang of remaining Agent Orange, the highly toxic defoliant used in the Vietnam War by U.S. forces. In June, President Nguyen Minh Triet makes first visit to the US by a Vietnamese head of state.

2008   The border dispute with China is resolved.

2011   In June, Vietnam begins joint operation with the United States to clean up contamination from Agent Orange.

Present Vietnam has followed China in liberalizing its economic policies. Nguyen has commented that it is "one of the great ironies and one of the great surprises of history ... that it's now sort of a state-run capitalism." Nevertheless, Vietnam continues to suppress free expression and to control access to information; political dissent is not tolerated. Nguyen has said, " [I]t's still a politically restrictive country. There is no free speech. There is limited freedom of religion." He added that *The*

Sympathizer could not officially be translated into Vietnamese because of the way it portrays the communists. ("Interview with Charlie Rose")

Acknowledgement: The above timeline draws on a number of sources including, but not limited to: Wikipedia, BBC News, History and Ducksters.

Introduction to Significant Characters

The **narrator** (**captain** or **sympathizer**) is an unnamed Vietnamese communist sympathizer whose political loyalties constantly clash with his personal loyalties. He was both in North Vietnam, the son of a French priest and a poor Vietnamese peasant girl. His ethnically mixed heritage means that he is frequently called a "bastard" in the country of his birth, and as an Asian he is never fully accepted as an American in the States.

Recruited to the communist cause in his youth by his close friend Man, he has kept his pro-communist allegiance secret. He spends six years at Occidental College, California, so he speaks American-English fluently and has a deep understanding of American culture. After completing his education, he returns to South Vietnam ostensibly to fight for the Republic against the communist North. He becomes a captain in the South Vietnamese Army, where he works for years as an under-cover spy in the role of aide-de-camp to the General. After having been evacuated from Saigon in the last hours before its fall, he is resettled in California and gets a job as a clerical assistant in the Department of Oriental Studies in the same college where he studied.

In California, he lives with his other great friend Bon and continues to assist the General. This leads him to work as a consultant on a Vietnam War film called *The Hamlet* and ultimately to return to Vietnam ostensibly to engage in counter-communist activity, although his real reason for going is to try to save the life of his friend Bon. The narrator is captured on his first mission and taken to a prison camp where he is forced to spend a year writing his confessions. Then he meets the camp Commissar (Man) who superintends the final stages of his reeducation. Finally, through Man's intervention, he and Bon are able to escape from Vietnam.

The General, who is the head of the Police Force in the Republic of Vietnam, is unnamed. As the Communist forces close in on Saigon, he arranges with a CIA agent for a plane to take his family and selected members of his staff out of the country. After resettlement in the USA, he opens a liquor store on Hollywood Boulevard, Los Angeles. He heads a military resistance movement that aims to reinvade and bring down the communist government of Vietnam.

Madam is the General's wife. They have five children, four in their teens in 1975 and one, a daughter, who is slightly older is studying in America. In California, Madam opens a small but successful restaurant.

Lan (who changes her name to **Lana** in America) is the General's eldest whom the narrator knew when she was a child before she went to study art history at the University of California at Berkley. After graduating, she becomes a singer. When they come to California, her mother and father are outraged by her way of life but are powerless to control her. The narrator is very attracted to Lana.

Claude is the CIA agent who arranges the General's escape and later himself gets out of Saigon just before its fall. He has spent several decades in Asia fighting the growth of communism, and it was he who identified the narrator as an able recruit to the Southern cause in 1954 when he was a nine-year-old refugee from the North. Claude escapes from Saigon almost at the last moment and in Los Angeles renews his contact with the General whom he sees as a potential leader of an insurgency against the communists in Vietnam. He is last encountered in Thailand supporting the anti-communist rebels in their secret incursions into Vietnam.

Man, Bon and the **protagonist** are three childhood friends, sworn blood brothers who think of themselves as the Three Musketeers.

Man is the narrator's secret communist spy-master in Vietnam. He gives the captain his mission to go to California to provide intelligence on the refugees, but he himself stays in Vietnam after the fall of Saigon to help the communists to rebuild the country. We later learn that he was hideously disfigured in a napalm blast. He continues to receive the captain's secret messages from California and when the captain intimates that he will return to Vietnam with Bon, Man orders him not to do so. Man turns out to be the Commissar of the prison camp to which the captain and Bon are taken after they are captured. He supervises the captain's reeducation, but eventually secures his release and that of Bon.

Bon is a "genuine patriot," his father having been publically executed by communists in the village square (15). Bon's wife, **Linh**, is a poet. They have one son, **Dun**, who is the narrator's godson. Linh and Dun are killed during the evacuation of Saigon. Bon lives with the captain in Los Angeles, but for over a year he is deeply depressed by the death of his wife and son. When the General orders the narrator to kill the major, it is Bon who actually pulls the trigger; when the General orders the narrator to kill Sonny, it is Bon who plans how he should do it. He returns to Vietnam to join the anti-communist insurgents, determined to get himself killed, but along with the captain he is taken captive and subjected to reeducation – a euphemism for torture.

The crapulent major ['crapulent' means 'relating to the drinking of alcohol or drunkenness'] is another who makes it out of Saigon on the General's plane. A year later, the narrator and Bon kill him (Bon actually fires the shot) after the captain has named him (to throw suspicion off himself) as a suspected spy for the communists feeding information to them about the refugees in California.

Mimi, Phi Phi and **Ti Ti** are three Vietnamese prostitutes whom the narrator knows. They are saved by an "American who actually kept his promises," a US sergeant who rescues as many girls as want to leave (39).

Avery Wright Hammer is the professor who supervised the protagonist's senior thesis. When he returns to California as an evacuee, the professor provides financial and other help including a job as clerical assistant at his old university.

The Department Chair is the head of Oriental Studies at the university where the captain works in Los Angeles.

Ms Sofia Mori is the secretary of the Department of Oriental Studies. Initially, the captain feels that she does not like him – ironically because she sympathizes with the communists and sees him as having fought against them. Soon, however, they become lovers, though she warns him that she is not looking for a committed relationship. Born in California, she is the daughter of Japanese immigrants, but sees herself as entirely American. During the captain's absence for the filming of *The Hamlet*, she and Sonny become lovers.

Son Do (Sonny) was a left-wing student whom the narrator met in 1969 when he was at college. At that time he "led the antiwar faction of Vietnamese foreign students" (93). The narrator meets him again at the opening of the General's liquor story which he is covering for the Vietnamese newspaper he edits. The narrator writes that Sonny, "Like a hard-core conservative … was right about everything. Or thought himself so, the key difference being that he was a naked leftist" (93). He uses his newspaper to criticize the General's plans for an anticommunist insurgency. The General orders the narrator to kill him and since Sonny has taken his mistress from him, the captain complies.

The Auteur is a movie director/producer working on a film called *The Hamlet* about Green Berets saving villagers in Vietnam. He angrily rejects the sympathizer's ideas about making the movie a more realistic presentation of the Vietnamese people. Later, however, he relents and offers him a job supervising the presentation of Vietnamese people in the shooting of the movie. This leads to further friction between the two and when the captain is injured in an explosion on set there is a rumor (never substantiated) that this is the director's way of getting his revenge.

Violet is his assistant.

Several members of the cast of *The Hamlet* are named.

Guiding Questions with notes and commentary

The questions are designed to focus your attention on the text whether you are reading it for the first time or rereading it. The aim is not to test you but to help you to understand the text. The questions do not normally have simple answers, nor is there always one answer. Consider a range of possible interpretations – preferably by discussing the questions with others. Disagreement is encouraged!

Chapter 1

1. What does the narrator mean when he writes, "I am ... a man of two faces ... I am also a man of two minds"?
2. Explain the complex relationship between the blood-brothers Man, Bon and the narrator.

Note: The story of the woman communist arrested in possession of a list of the names of the General's entire staff will later be very important in the novel.

Notes

"a spy, a sleeper, a spook" (1): Three alliterative synonyms. A sleeper agent is a spy who goes under-cover in another country or organization, sometimes for years, to gain the enemy's trust in order to destroy it. Spook is a slang term for a spy (presumably because spies are about as hard to find as ghosts).

"April, the cruelest month" (1): A reference to the opening lines of *The Waste Land* (1922) by the American poet T. S. Eliot (1888-1965):

> April is the cruellest month, breeding
> Lilacs out of the dead land, mixing
> Memory and desire, stirring
> Dull roots with spring rain.
> Winter kept us warm, covering
> Earth in forgetful snow, feeding
> A little life with dried tubers.

"Bourgogne" (2): Red Burgundy wine, which is supposed to be drunk at room temperature.

"foreign Svengalis" (2): The name Svengali comes from a character in the novel *Trilby* (1895) by George du Maurier (1834-1896). Svengali uses hypnotic powers to establish control over Trilby O'Ferrall, the novel's heroine.

"our northern brethren" (2): North Vietnam, officially the Democratic Republic of Vietnam (DRV), came into being in 1954. On September 2nd, 1945, under Hồ Chí Minh, Vietnam declared its independence from French Indochina. This led to a decade-long war which only ended in 1954 when the French were defeated. Vietnam was divided into the North, which was communist, and the South, which was not. North Vietnam attempted to unify the country by force, leading to the Vietnam War (1955–75).

"Karl Marx, V. I. Lenin, and Chairman Mao" (2): Karl Marx (1818-1883),

German political philosopher who predicted the overthrow of capitalism by the proletariat (workers) and the establishment of a classless, communist society. Vladimir Ilyich Ulyanov (1870-1924), Russian communist revolutionary who was head of the government of Soviet Russia from the Revolution in 1917 until his death in 1924. He established the Soviet Union as a one-party state governed by the Russian Communist Party. Mao Zedong (1893-1976) led communist forces to victory over the nationalists in the Chinese civil war and was Chairman of the Communist Party of China from its establishment in 1949 until his death in 1976. His attempts to change Chinese society and the economy of the country led to millions of deaths and much suffering.

"*The Communist Manifesto*" (3): Originally titled *Manifesto of the Communist Party* (1848), this was co-written by Karl Marx and Friedrich Engels (1820-1895). Basing its analysis of past and present societies on the assertion that "The history of all hitherto existing society is the history of class struggles," it predicts the eventual overthrow of capitalism and the establishment of a classless, socialist society.

"Mao's *Little Red Book*" (3): Mao Zedong's *Little Red Book: Quotations from Chairman Mao Zedong* is a compilation of 267 quotations from the Chinese leader's speeches and writings. During the Cultural Revolution in China (1966-1976), in which millions were persecuted or killed, conformity with Mao's thought was necessary for survival.

"Nikolay Chernyshevsky" (3): Nikolay Gavrilovich Chernyshevsky (1828-1889), Russian philosopher and novelist who led the revolutionary democratic movement of the 1860s. Arrested in 1862, he wrote the pro-socialist novel *What Is to Be Done?* (1863).

"*mission civilisatrice*" (3): Meaning "civilizing mission" – a concept used by Western nations to justify colonization and exploitation for four centuries.

"our northern front had collapsed" (3): On March 10th, 1975, North Vietnamese General Dung launched Campaign 275, an assault on the Central Highlands of South Vietnam which met very little resistance. By March 30th, the key city of Da Nang and the defense of the Central Highlands and Northern provinces had completely collapsed. The way was now open for the North to take the capital of the South, Saigon, which it did on April 30th.

"our president, Thieu" (3): Nguyễn Văn Thiệu (1923-2001) was president of South Vietnam from 1965 to 1975. He resigned on April 21st when it was clear that South Vietnam was indefensible. With the help of the CIA, Thieu escaped and lived out his life in England and later the U.S.A.

"spurned our request to send more money" (4): All U.S. forces were withdrawn from South Vietnam by March 1973 following the signing of the Paris Peace Accords on January 27th, 1973. In August 1974, Congress voted to cut financial aid to South Vietnam from $1 billion to $700 million a year.

"Beethoven" (5): Ludwig van Beethoven (1770-1827), the classical German composer. As I understand it, there is some evidence that Beethoven's mother, Magdalena Keverich, had Moorish ancestry, but the question remains unresolved.

"CIA … OSS" (5): The Office of Strategic Services (O.S.S.) was a wartime intelligence agency of the United States formed in 1942 during World War II and terminated by President Truman in 1945. The Central Intelligence Agency (C.I.A.), formed in 1947, is a civilian foreign intelligence service of the American government.

"Richard Hedd's *Asian Communism and the Oriental Mode of Destruction … On Understanding and Defeating the Marxist Threat in Asia*" (6): There was/is no such book. It is a fictionalized text that Lisa Locascio describes as "an essentialist treatise that the narrator uses as both cipher and key to encode his communications with fellow spy Man and decode the narratives with which he has been programmed and the categories in which he has been placed" (Bookforum.com).

"Moses, as played by Charlton Heston" (6): In the 1956 religious epic movie *The Ten Commandments*, the part of Moses was played by Charlton Heston (1923-2008) an iconic actor and political conservative.

"C130" (6): Lockheed C-130 Hercules, a four-engine turboprop military transport aircraft in service throughout the Vietnam War.

"Jane Fonda" (7): Jane Seymour Fonda (born 1937), American actress who strongly opposed the Vietnam War. In July 1972, she visited Hanoi, capital of North Vietnam, where she criticized American bombing. A photograph of Fonda seated on an anti-aircraft gun generated a great deal of hostility in the U.S.; Fonda was given the name "Hanoi Jane" by those who saw her as a traitor.

"Peoria or Poughkeepsie" (8): Peoria is in Illinois; Poughkeepsie is in New York.

"Fort Benning" (12): A large US Army post on the Alabama-Georgia border.

"Green Berets" (12): Established in 1952, the United States Army Special Forces are named for the color of the beret they wear. *The Green Berets* (1968) is film set in Vietnam which defends the U.S. intervention in the country's civil war. It was directed by and starred John Wayne (1907-1979).

"Occidental … *Occidens Proximus Orienti*" (12): Occidental College is a private liberal arts college in Los Angeles, California. Its motto is: 'The West is nearest the East.'

"Emerson" (12): Ralph Waldo Emerson (1803-1882), American philosopher who consistently supported the rights of the individual against the pressures of the group (i.e., society, the body politic).

"Minox mini-camera" (14): Every spy's favorite camera, the Minox was made of stainless steel and measured 3-4x1x0.5 inches.

"phrenological purpose" (14): Phrenology was a pseudo-science which claimed that clues to the personality of a person could be gained from examining the shape and structure of his/her skull.

"Guam" (15): The island of Guam in the western Pacific Ocean is the westernmost territory of the United States. Andersen Air Force Base on Guam was used for bombing operations during the Vietnam War.

"Marcos" (15): Ferdinand Emmanuel Edralin Marcos Sr. (1917-1989), President of the Philippines from 1965 to 1986, was a corrupt and brutal dictator.

"Trinh Cong Son" (16): Trịnh Công Sơn (1939-2001) famous Vietnamese artist, songwriter and musician

"Dumas" (16): Alexandre Dumas (1802-1870) wrote *The Three Musketeers* (1844) a historical adventure set in the reign of King Louis XIV. Dumas's father was the son of a French nobleman and a female slave of African descent.

"Erle Stanley Gardner" (16): American lawyer and author (1889-1970) famous for his novels featuring defense attorney Perry Mason.

Commentary

The narrative is in the first person. From the complex sentence structures and the careful phrasing, it appears to be a written rather than a spoken or stream of consciousness narrative. It uses both the past and the present tenses. The narrator assumes that the person reading his narrative (it is very quickly evident that the narrator is male) will have a great deal of background information that the reader of the novel does not, in fact, have. As a result, we are thrust right into the middle of a situation and left by the author to make sense of it for ourself. Specifically, the reader has to answer three questions: Where is the narrator now? What was the narrator's role in the events of the past that he describes? How are these two things related? The first two questions are resolved in this chapter while the third is not fully resolved until the end of the novel.

The unnamed protagonist calls his narrative a "confession" addressed to the "Commandant" of the prison in which he is currently held (2). Since the Commandant knows the background to the narrator's story, the narrator plunges straight into it without explanation: he does nor even identify South Vietnam as the setting, or the year as 1975. He contrasts his present isolation cell with the room in the General's villa that he occupied during the Vietnam War when he was aide-de-camp to the head of the National Police with the rank of captain. He tells the story of the rapid collapse of resistance in South Vietnam beginning in March 1975 up to the preparations that were made with the help of the C.I.A. to evacuate the General, his family and selected members of his staff (including the narrator) just before the fall of Saigon. It seems reasonable to suppose that he is currently being held in a communist prison where he is being interrogated about his part in the Revolution, though when and how he was captured is not clear.

It also becomes clear that, for several years before 1975, the protagonist had been a communist spy recruited and handled by his friend Man. In this capacity, he spent "six idyllic years" in a California college where he gained a Masters degree and became fully conversant with all aspects of American history and culture. This makes his current incarceration by the communists puzzling. However, there was one incident in which he conspicuously failed: a woman who he was using to pass information to Man was arrested with the names of everyone on the General's staff. Not only did the captain fail to get a warning to her, he also failed to save her from being interrogated (i.e., tortured). He clearly feels the guilt of his failures.

The narrator is of mixed race and is illegitimate (his father being a French priest and his mother a poor peasant girl). He is sensitive about his status and reacts emotionally whenever he is called a "bastard" – which he is rather frequently. His race is why he identifies with Beethoven and with Dumas, a quadroon (a person one-quarter black). He has two close friends, Man and Bon, whom he regards as blood brothers. However, the relationship is complicated because while Bon is a supporter of the South, both Man and the protagonist are communists – something they hide from Bon.

The first thing that the protagonist confesses is, "I am a man of two minds … I am simply able to see any issue from both sides" (1). He then adds that this is less a talent (a skill one controls and uses) than a hazard (a tendency that one cannot control). He identifies his own bi-racial origin as the source of his ability to see both sides of every issue (or say rather his inability to see just one side). Thus, despite being a sleeper agent for the communists, he "could not help but feel moved by the plight of … [the] poor people" caught in the communist offensive (3). He comments, "Perhaps it was not correct, politically speaking, for me to feel sympathy for them, but my mother would have been one of them if she were alive" (3). Similarly, he identifies with the young soldiers of the South who "sensed that within days they would be dead … They were my enemies, and yet they were my brothers-in-arms" (17). Now it makes sense why he should be imprisoned and interrogated by the communists for they demand complete adherence to the party orthodoxy, and the protagonist is not capable of that.

Chapter 2

3. Explain the protagonist's "muddled heritage" (21). How has his experience as an outsider impacted his political development?
Note: The captain writes that the General "never sneered about my muddled heritage" Remember that statement about the General. It will be important much later in the narrative
4. Explain why the narrator is going to the U.S.A. Why is Man staying in Vietnam? Why is Bon escaping to the U.S.A.?
Note: Remember the communist slogan, "'Nothing is more precious than independence and freedom'" (27). It will recur frequently in the narrative and will be very important to the climax of the novel.

Notes
"métis" (20): Half-caste.
"Le Cercle Sportif" (20): The Saigon Sports Circle Athletic Club was officially established in 1906. Its extensive sports facilities made it a fashionable

rendezvous for the elite of colonial society. (It is now the Labour Culture Palace.)
"Pernod" (20): One of the most popular French liqueurs.
"Dien Bien Phu" (23): This battle occurred between March and May 1954. It resulted in a comprehensive French defeat which led directly to the signing of the 1954 Geneva Accords by which France agreed to withdraw from all its colonies in French Indochina.
"Uncle Ho" (27): Hồ Chí Minh (1890-1969) led the Việt Minh independence movement from 1941. He was President of the Communist-ruled Democratic Republic of Vietnam from 1945 to 1969. Following its capture, Saigon, former capital of the Republic of Vietnam, was renamed Hồ Chí Minh City.
"Trotskyist" (28): A follower of Leon Trotsky (1879-1940) one of the founders of the Communist U.S.S.R. who was exiled from the Soviet Union in February 1929 because of his opposition to Stalin's policies. In exile, Trotsky continued to oppose Stalinist rule in the Soviet Union until he was assassinated.
"arrondissement" (28): An administrative subdivision.
"since '73" (32): Following the Paris Peace Accords, the U.S. completed its military withdrawal from South Vietnam. By July 30th, there were fewer than 250 members of the U.S. military in South Vietnam, excluding the marines guarding the American Embassy in Saigon.
"Moro warriors" (33): The Moro are the Muslim population of the Philippines. From 1899 to 1913, the Moro rebelled against the U.S. forces during the Philippine-American War. They were defeated.
"Phoenix Program" (35): A U.S.-led program designed "to identify and destroy the Viet Cong (VC) via infiltration, capture, counter-terrorism, interrogation, and assassination. The CIA described it as 'a set of programs that sought to attack and destroy the political infrastructure of the Viet Cong'" (Wikipedia article).
"Katyusha rockets" (35): A Soviet mobile unguided rocket-launching system.

Commentary

The narrator is obviously troubled by his own Eurasian heritage and by the hateful words that he is so often called. One reason for his being drawn to the General is that he judges him by his efficiency and "never sneered about my muddled heritage" (21). [*Note:* Remember that statement about the General. It will be important much later in the narrative.] In organizing the evacuation, the captain reveals his organizational skill and particularly his "ability to finesse the fine line between the legal and the illegal" (21). Of the General he says, "he was a sincere man who believed in everything he said, even if it was a lie, which makes him not so different from most" (23). Here the lie the General tells (and believes) is that he will return to fight for the liberation of South Vietnam from the Communists – that will never happen.

The captain recalls his education in communist ideology by his friend Man who ran a secret study group. Man stressed the need for total subservience to "the tenets of Party ideology" among which was the communist slogan, "'Nothing is more precious than independence and freedom'" (27). [*Note:* This slogan will also be very important to the climax of the novel.] This saying helps us to understand the uncompromising demand of the Party to loyalty. Nevertheless, in his confession, the captain reports that, even in the last hours of the war, he could not help but see the moral equivalence of the two sides. What makes the protagonist different is that he belongs neither in Vietnam nor in America – he is out of place in both and cannot therefore take one side or the other. He writes of the warring communists and nationalists, "all saw themselves as patriots fighting for a country to which they belonged" (30).

Even the major whom he has bribed to let the bus through to the airport keeps his end of the bargain. The captain comments approvingly, "Although he could have shot me, or turned us back, he did what I gambled every honorable man forced to take a bribe would do. He let us all pass, holding up his end of the bargain..." (31-32). Quite evidently, this would be regarded by the Party as counter-revolutionary thinking, so the Commandant would certainly not agree that "It is always better to admire the best among our foes rather than the worst among our friends" (32). This is moral relativism.

There is a marked contrast between the chaotic situation around Saigon and the efficiency of the network of communist cells of which the protagonist is a small part. For the Americans, the evacuation is "A mess ... Situation normal, all fucked up" (33). It hardly seems surprising that the North won the war – they are so much better at war than are either the Americans or the South Vietnamese.

Chapter 3

5. Explain why the Commandant asks the protagonist what he means by writing "'we' or 'us'" when referring to "the southern soldiers and evacuees" upon whom he was sent to spy by the communists (36)? What is his answer?

6. Speaking of the cease-fire that followed the Paris Accords of 1973, the narrator writes:

> It was a smashingly successful cease-fire, for in the last two years only 150,000 soldiers had died, in addition to the requisite number of civilians. Imagine how many would have died without a truce! (41)

How would you describe the tone of this statement? How do you react to this statement?

7. Describe how the tone of the narrative changes from the moment when a rocket explodes destroying the plane on which the evacuees are escaping? (See bottom of page 43.)

Notes

"Clark Kent ... Superman ... Smallville" (38): Mild-mannered Kent is the alter ego of Superman. Behind the identity of this reporter for the Daily Planet newspaper in Smallville, Superman can blend in.

"C130s" (40): The Lockheed C-130 Hercules is a four-engine turboprop military transport aircraft which saw service throughout the Vietnam War.

"ICCS" (40): The International Commission of Control and Supervision (I.C.C.S.) was created after the Paris Peace Accords were signed on January 27th, 1973, to monitor compliance with the cease-fire terms of that agreement. Specifically, its remit was: to supervise the implementation of the cease-fire; to monitor the withdrawal of troops and the dismantlement of military bases; to check on activity at ports of entry; and to facilitate the return of prisoners of war and captured foreign civilians. The 1,160 personnel of the commission were from Canada, Hungary, Indonesia and Poland. On the evidence of history, the cease-fire was ignored by the North and the I.C.C.S. was pretty ineffective.

"M16" (43): The M16 rifle was introduced in 1964 and was extensively used by US forces in jungle warfare operations during the Vietnam War. It could fire up to 950 rounds a minute.

"Chinook" (44): The Boeing CH-47 Chinook is a twin-engine helicopter introduced in 1962. It is capable of lifting heavy loads.

"NVA" (45): The North Vietnamese Army, also known as the People's Army of Vietnam (P.A.V.N.), the Vietnamese People's Army (V.P.A.), and the Việt Minh.

"Ngo Dinh Diem" (46): Ngô Đình Diệm (1901-1963) was a South Vietnamese politician. In 1955, following a corrupt referendum, he established himself as president of the first Republic of Vietnam (RVN). Diệm was deposed and assassinated during a C.I.A.-backed coup in November 1963.

"Rorschach blot" (46): In a Rorschach test, a person's perceptions of a series of random inkblots are recorded and then analyzed. This is thought to give an indication of the subject's mental processes and personality.

"kamikaze pilot" (48): As Japan began to lose World War II, suicide pilots crashed their aircraft loaded with explosives into enemy targets. The tactic was a failure since Japan quickly ran out of trained pilots.

"AK47" (48): The Kalashnikov rifle – a Soviet-made assault rifle.

"Shadow gunship" (49): The Fairchild AC-119G Shadow – a ground-attack aircraft introduced into service late in 1968.

Commentary

The Commandant has objected to the captain's use of the first person plural ('we' and 'us') to describe his feelings about "the southern soldiers and evacuees" whom he saw during his last hours in Saigon (36). To a communist, these people are enemies (the third person plural 'them') for whom 'we' can have no sympathy at all. Although he admits it to be a "weakness," the narrator links his inability to see the defending soldiers as enemies with his mixed race, "being a bastard naturally predisposes one to sympathy" and credits his "gentle mother for teaching me the idea that blurring the lines between us and them can be a worthy behavior" (36).

The narrator's bitterness comes across in his description of the period after the Paris Accords when the U.S. forces pulled out of the country. Note the bitter sarcasm in his tone:

> It was a smashingly successful cease-fire, for in the last two years only 150,000 soldiers had died, in addition to the requisite number of civilians. Imagine how many would have died without a truce! (41)

The word "smashingly" (with its childish connotations) is comic hyperbole, but it also carries connotations of the destruction that came in the wake of the cease-fire. The word "requisite" used to describe the number of civilian dead is bitterly ironic, as though some heartless bureaucrat had calculated the 'right' number of civilian deaths. The narrator's message is that the cease-fire was a sham from the start, and that the U.S. acted in bad faith by using it as a pretext to abandon the people in South Vietnam whom they had promised to protect.

The description of waiting to be called at the airport stresses the boredom and inconvenience of the experience. There are not enough toilets for the evacuees, and so they use the previously segregated swimming pool – more ironic humor. However, when a rocket hits the C130 as it is preparing for take-off, the tone of the description changes to one of real fear and anxiety. It suddenly occurs to the escaping Vietnamese that they might *not* be able to get airborne before the communist forces take the airfield. When another C130 lands, everyone at the airport realizes that it will be the last plane out and each person there wants to be on it. In the scramble, Linh and Duc are killed by the same bullet and the chapter ends with a terrible description of Bon's grief. The deaths of these entirely sympathetic characters so early in the novel is unexpected, alerting the reader that this novel is going to deal with its subject with honest realism.

Chapter 4

8. The protagonist writes, "I was ... one of those unfortunate cases who could not help but wonder whether my need for American charity was due to my having first been the recipient of American aid" (62). Explain what he means by this. Having been, in his opinion, let down by the Americans, the captain is a harsh critic of U.S. foreign policy in Vietnam. Do you find his statement justifiable?
9. Comment on the lists that the narrator makes in response to his Chair's suggestion. When the Chair comments, "A fine beginning," what does he mean about how the narrator should adapt to living in the U.S.A. (64)?

Notes

"Camp Pendleton" (55): A major Marine Base in San Diego County, Southern California. "In 1975 Camp Pendleton was the first military base in the US to provide accommodations for Vietnamese evacuees in Operation New Arrivals; over 50,000 refugees came to the base in the largest humanitarian airlift in history" (Wikipedia article).

"steganography" (55): The act of concealing secret messages within or alongside a non-secret text.

"Graham Greene" (58): Henry Graham Greene (1904-1991), prolific and important English writer. His novel *The Quiet American* (1955) depicts the end of French colonialism in Vietnam and anticipates the Americans coming in to fill the vacuum left by the French withdrawal.

"Everlasting Church of Prophets" (59): There *is* a Church of the Everlasting God and all His Prophets, but it seems to be a twenty-first century movement.

"a slightly less tony part of Los Angeles" (59): That is, a slightly less stylish or luxurious part of the city.

"IRS" (60): The Internal Revenue Service which deals with taxes and such.

"*NLF*" (61): The National Liberation Front of South Vietnam (or Việt Cộng) was established by the North in December 1960 to subvert and bring down the government of South Vietnam and thus reunify the country under communist rule.

"tchotchkes" (62): Small decorative objects; trinkets.

"Taiwan … Mao" (63): Taiwan is a large island to the east of the People's Republic of China (P.R.C.) which calls itself the Republic of China (R.O.C.). Following a civil war between the nationalists, led by Chiang Kai-shek (1887-1975), and the communists, led by Mao Zedong, the R.O.C. was expelled from the mainland and established its government in Taiwan in 1949. It is still there.

"perineum" (67): The area between the anus and the scrotum or vulva.

"the grand cru of Phu Quoc Island" (70): A Vietnamese island in the Gulf of Thailand famous for its sauce. A 'cru' is a French vineyard producing wine grapes – by extensions Phu Quoc produces fish sauce.

"Tippi Hedren" (71): Nathalie Kay 'Tippi' Hedren (born 1930) is an American actress who took a very active interest in assisting Vietnamese refugees in the U.S.A. particularly by training women to work in, and eventually own, nail salons.

Commentary

This chapter deals with the resettlement of Vietnamese refugees in the America. It is not a positive picture. The narrator gets a minimum wage job at his old college; Bon has a part-time job as watchman at a church, but is paid off the books so that he can also collect welfare (which is common amongst the refugees); the General opens a liquor store. The chapter ends with a long list of people who failed to make it in the States balanced by a few stories of those who did.

The General begins to suspect that the communists have sleeper agents amongst the evacuee community sending intelligence back to Vietnam (which is, ironically precisely what the captain is doing). In order to deflect suspicion from himself, the captain suggests that the "crapulous major" may be the spy (58), but the relocation of the General's family, Bon and the captain to Los Angeles takes the General's mind off his fears and the matter is dropped.

The narrator's mixed ethnicity continues to be an issue. His Department

Chair tells him, "You must assiduously cultivate those reflexes that Americans have learned innately, in order to counterweight your Oriental instincts" (65). This way (by effectively suppressing his Asian side) he can "learn how not to be torn apart" by his opposing sides. The narrator points out that he is Eurasian not Amerasian, but the Chair does not find the distinction important. Nguyen has said that the character of the Chair of Oriental Studies is a comic satirical caricature.

On the first anniversary of the communist victory, the protagonist cannot help but see the event from every side. He refers to "Saigon's fall, or liberation, or both" adding, "I confess that I could not help but feel pity for my sorry countrymen, their germs of loss passed back and forth until I, too, walked around light-headed in the fog of memory" (68). Certainly this is a confession, but the Commandant will not understand how the captain still feels this way.

Chapter 5

10. We have now heard quite a lot about the narrator's confinement and the confession he is making. Explain your ideas about where he currently is and how he might have got there.

11. The narrator says that some will find his story of the squid "obscene" (80). Do you? Why/why not? Explain why the narrator does *not* find it obscene?

Notes

"*Ooga booga*" (74): A primitive form of greeting – 'caveman' talk.

"*cracker*" (74): A slang term for a backward, uneducated, conservative poor white (particularly in Florida) comparable to the slur 'redneck.' In this context, it means the Vietnamese equivalent.

"gaijin" (74): In Japan, 'a foreigner.'

"Suzie Wong" (74): A good-hearted Chinese prostitute in the novel *The World of Suzie Wong* (1957) by British novelist Richard Mason (1919-1997). The book was made into a movie in 1960 with William Holden as the leading man. Nancy 'Ka Shen' Kwan (born 1939), a Hong Kong-born American actress, played Suzie Wong.

"William Holden ... Marlon Brando ... Mickey Rooney" (74): Holden (1918-1981) and Brando (1924-2004) were handsome movie stars; Rooney (1920-2014) was a comic actor. All are Caucasian.

"*Karma Sutra* or *The Carnal Prayer Mat*" (75): Respectively an ancient Hindu sex manual and a 17th-century Chinese erotic novel.

"Gardena" (75): A city in the South Bay region of Los Angeles County, California.

"nisei" (75): Person born in the U.S. or Canada whose parents were immigrants from Japan.

"issei" (75): Japanese immigrant to North America.

"Confucian" (76): Relating to Confucius (551-479 BC) or the philosophy of Confucianism. "In sexual matters, Confucianism is quite 'puritanic.' A 'good young girl is not only expected to keep her virginity until she gets married and to get married only once in her life, she is not supposed to make herself attractive, even to her own husband." In fact, this attitude to sex only developed long after the death of Confucius himself. (Confucian Beliefs, factsanddetails.com)

"sybarite" (77): Voluptuary; a sensualist who enjoys physical pleasure.
"onanism" (78): Masturbation.
"odalisque" (79): Female slave or concubine in a harem.
"snafu" (85): A chaotic mess.
".38 Special" (89): Small revolver favored by police.

Commentary

Where is the narrator and to whom is he making his confession? My guess (and it is no more than that since I wrote this sentence during my first reading of the novel) is that the protagonist has returned to Vietnam and has been arrested for having pro-American sympathies. Perhaps the communists who are holding him believe (irony of ironies) that he is a secret agent for the Americans sent over to spy on them.

One thing is for certain, the authorities holding him do not share his ability to see both sides of a political/military question. That, of course, could apply to both the American and the Vietnamese governments. The captain writes, "I cannot blame you for the unusual qualities of my confession … I am guilty of honesty…" (72).

Sofia Mori is the daughter of Japanese immigrants. She was born in California and feels not attachment at all to Japanese culture – something that shocks and disappoints the Chair of Studies for whom she works. Unlike the narrator, Sofia knows who she is; she tells him, "I damn well know my culture, which is American, and my language, which is English" (76).

The narrator expresses his views on human sexuality. He says that for him "the seed of sexual rebellion one day matured into … political rebellion" (78) and that his affair with Sofia taught him that "true revolution also involved sexual liberation" (77). This is another point on which the Commandant would find him to be in error.

The sympathizer includes details of his own childhood self-pleasuring (masturbation). Some readers will find the story of the squid hilarious and others offensive. The narrator has played a trick on the censorious reader. He tells us passionately that his account of self-pleasuring is not "obscene … Massacre is obscene. Torture is obscene. Three million dead is obscene" (80). This story is immediately followed by Claude's horrific account of the chaotic evacuation of Saigon in which hundreds of South Vietnamese who had collaborated with the Americans and been promised an escape were simply left behind. We really have no alternative but to adjust our values and agree that "the world would be a better place if the word 'murder' made us mumble as much as the word 'masturbation'" (80). The Commandant, however, is not a man to adjust his values; whichever

25

side he is on, he sees things in absolute terms.

The description of the horror of the evacuation is followed by a description of its absurd comedy: the secret signal for the evacuation (the playing of "'White Christmas'" on the radio) was known to "everyone in the city"; at the crucial moment the deejay could not find the right version of the song; the evacuation was designated "Frequent Wind," a name that brought to mind flatulence so that "all the bad air whipped up by the American helicopters was the equivalent of a massive blast of gas in the faces of those left behind" (85). The narrator's bitterness at the Americans' incompetence and lack of empathy for the Vietnamese is expressed in his bitter sarcasm.

One theme revisited in this chapter is the captain's claim that he "never used violence insomuch as I allowed others to use it in front of me" (80). He admits to being tortured by the memory of those he saw interrogated, including the woman arrested with the list of names in her mouth. He writes, "the memories of those whom I had seen interrogated continued to hijack me with fatal persistence" (80). He is in the same position when it comes to executing the major (whom he knows to be innocent): he will plan the hit, but Bon is the one who will actually fire the gun. This evasion of responsibility may be one of the things that the Commandant is trying to get the captain to acknowledge through his confession, because, of course, in the Commandant's view a fighter committed to the cause (whether that be communist or anti-communist) should have no hesitation to commit murder nor suffer bad conscience for having done so.

Chapter 6

12. Contrast Claude's view of killing the crapulent major (102-103) with that of the narrator.

13. What aspect of the shooting does not go as the sympathizer had planned it? Why is this so important to him?

Notes

"Richard Nixon" (92): Richard Milhous Nixon (1913-1994), President of the United States from 1969 until he resigned in 1974. In the early years of his presidency, the U.S. escalated operations against North Vietnam including massive bombing of the civilian population.

"John Wayne" (92): Marion Robert Morrison (1907-1979), a popular movie actor famous for his patriotic portrayal of the U.S. military, for example in *The Green Berets* (1968) produced at the height of the Vietnam War.

"Agent Orange" (92): A defoliant chemical used during the Vietnam War from 1961 to 1971 to deny the Viet Cong jungle cover. It caused severe health problems to those exposed to it.

"Gauguin" (92): Eugène Henri Paul Gauguin (1848-1903), influential French artist of the post-Impressionist school.

"Poulo Condore" (94): Côn Đảo Prison on Côn Sơn Island (off the south east coast of Vietnam) was built by the French in 1861 to house political prisoners. It was turned over to the government of South Vietnam in 1954. During the Vietnam War, the prison was notorious for its brutal torture of prisoners many of whom were chained in so-called 'tiger cages.'

"quotidian" (94): Ordinary, occurring every day; daily

"Walt Whitman" (94): Walter Whitman (1819-1892), American writer most famous for his poems *The Leaves of Grass*.

"Cholon" (95): Chợ Lớn is a district in Saigon.

"The Quiet American" (100): Written by English author Graham Greene (1904-1991) in 1955, the novel is set in French Colonial Vietnam. It describes the growing American involvement in Vietnam.

"Noël Coward" (101): Sir Noël Peirce Coward (1899-1973), multi-talented English writer and musician. He was generally known to be gay at a time when that was a criminal offence.

"Hegel" (102): Georg Wilhelm Friedrich Hegel (1770-1831), German philosopher.

"Bruce Lee" (104): Lee Jun-fan (1940 -1973), actor in and director of very popular martial arts movies.

"Sa Dec" (107): Sa Đéc is a large port city in the Mekong Delta of southern Vietnam.

"Bouncing Betty" (107): Colloquial name for the German S-mine which is planted in the ground. When triggered, it releases explosives which detonate in the air (hence 'bouncing') spraying deadly shrapnel.

Commentary

The narrator reviews the new lives of the evacuees: the men have been reduced to jobs they would have scorned in Vietnam; the women have been forced out to work; and their children are drifting away from their parents because they are adapting more quickly to American culture. The General has given the captain a task for which he is ill-suited: the murder of the "crapulent major" who is now a gas station attendant whose wife works sewing in a sweatshop. The sympathizer knows that the man is innocent since he suggested his name to the General only to divert attention and suspicion from himself. In conversation, he suggests that the major move away from Los Angeles, but the major rejects the idea. When he has breakfast with the major, the captain says he "could not help but love and pity the man in his innocence" (95).

Killing someone gives Bon's life meaning, which it has not had since the death of his wife and son. In contrast, the captain has avoided killing, even in Vietnam. He writes, "What I did not have was the desire or the various uniforms of justification a man dons as camouflage – the need to defend God, country, honor, ideology, or comrades … These off-the-rack excuses fit some people well, but not me" (98).

When he broaches the question of the major's possible innocence with

Claude, the C.I.A. man, we see the difference between the sympathizer and a man totally committed to a political cause. To Claude, there is no such thing as innocence; the major has probably got innocent people arrested, even murdered, proving to Claude that, "We're all innocent on one level and guilty on another" (103). Thinking like that justifies killing anyone. The captain is, however, unconvinced, "Original Sin was simply too unoriginal for someone like me, born of a father who spoke of it at every Mass" (103). He recalls an incident in Vietnam when the major had taken bribes from the wife of a man he had identified as Viet Cong and concludes, "the crapulent major was as sinful as Claude estimated" (106).

As we would expect, the sympathizer is both efficient and meticulous in planning the murder/assassination. He describes every detail of stalking the major to get to know his routine and refers to the agreed time of the shooting as "our appointment with the crapulous major," a euphemism that allows him to evade the harsh reality (104). However, the sympathizer cannot bring himself to fire the shot. Bon, whose anti-communist attitude is fixed and who needs to find a sense of purpose for his existence, has no reservations about shooting the major. Bon is supposed to shoot from behind so that the major knows nothing of what is happening. This is not to spare the major but to protect the narrator's feelings. However, at the last minute, Bon calls the major's name because he cannot bring himself to shoot the man in the back of the head. As a result, the sympathizer sees the major's face when he dies – he sees the third eye that the bullet creates in his forehead. Later, the captain cannot sleep, "No matter whether my eyes were open or shut, I could still see it, the crapulent major's third eye, weeping because of what it could see about me" (110). In fact, it is what the sympathizer can see about himself that keeps him awake; his conscience keeps him awake. From this point on, the captain cannot shake the 'ghost' of the major which haunts his imagination.

Chapter 7

14. In what ways is the narrator different from Man, the General and the Congressman? What do they have in common that he does not have?
15. Why does Lana's chosen lifestyle offend her father and mother so much?

Notes
"Clarke Gable" (112): William Clark Gable (1901-1960), American movie actor noted for his handsome looks.
"Louis XIV" (113): Louis the Great, or the Sun King (1638-1715), King of France from 1643 to 1715.
"Mae West" (113): Mary Jane 'Mae' West (1893-1980), American actress and comedian noted for her sexual suggestiveness.
"ao dai" (114): A traditional Vietnamese garment; a tight-fitting tunic, normally worn over trousers, with a high neck and long sleeves.

"'The Three Submissions and Four Virtues'" (115): The basic moral principles set out for women in Confucianism. A woman must *obey*: her father as daughter, her husband as wife, and her sons in widowhood. The four womanly virtues are: wifely virtue, wifely speech, wifely manner/appearance, and wifely work.

"Rita Hayworth" (122): Margarita Carmen Cansino (1918-1987), glamorous American actress and dancer. *Gilda* was released in 1946.

"Castro" (122): Fidel Alejandro Castro Ruz (1926-2016), led the communist revolution in Cuba and became head of government from 1959 to 2008.

"*The Hamlet*" (123): This fictional movie is based on *Apocalypse Now* (1979) directed, produced, and co-written by Francis Ford Coppola (born 1939).

"Audie Murphy" (123): Audie Leon Murphy (1925-1971), decorated American hero of World War II who became a popular movie actor particularly known for his roles in Westerns.

Commentary

There is a huge contrast in this chapter between the narrator and every other male character: *they* are single-minded in their opposition to communism (with the exception of Sonny whose sympathies are with the communists), while *he* inevitably sees two sides to every issue. Thus, he is "troubled" by the murder he has committed believing that the major was "a relatively innocent man, which is the best one could hope for in this world" – the very wording indicates that he can identify with the dead man (111). The sympathizer quiets his conscience by drinking too much, "Besides my conscience, my liver was the most abused part of my body" he jokes (114). He knows that Man would not be similarly troubled; for Man there are no innocent people, even revolutionaries. At the major's funeral, the General (the man who ordered the hit) slips the widow some money that has been provided by a C.I.A. operational fund – the General feels no hypocrisy.

The Congressman is another whose opposition to communism is absolute, though he is another character whom the narrator satirizes. Talking of the cause, he tells his Vietnamese audience, "America is the land of freedom and independence" (119). Sonny points out the irony that this is "the same slogan the Communist Party uses" (120). Although Sophia Mori concludes cynically that, "A slogan is an empty suit … Anyone can wear it" (120), this slogan allows the Congressman to convince himself that legislation to control the movies and the music industry "is not censorship, only advice with teeth" – an absurd oxymoron (123). Asked for his opinion of the Congressman, the captain tells Sonny, "He's the best thing that could have happened to us" (121). Ostensibly, "us" refers to the Vietnamese refugees because he is providing money for the resistance, but it could also refer to the communist Vietnamese since continued American aggression will keep the people's enthusiasm for the struggle high. It is "the best kind of truth, the one that meant at least two things" (121).

Lana, the General's daughter, is single-minded in a different way: she has put

Vietnamese ideas of the submissive role of women behind her and is seeking to forge a career as a singer. The captain finds himself sexually attracted to her – which could threaten his relationship with the General.

Chapter 8

16. Explain what the narrator finds so unsatisfactory about the screenplay for *The Hamlet*.
17. The narrator says that the war in Vietnam "was the first war where the losers would write history instead of the victors." Explain what he means by that. How valid do you find that observation?

Notes

"prelapsarian" (125): Innocent and unspoiled as man was in the Garden of Eden before the Fall.

"Montagnards" (125): Hill-dwelling people in the highlands of Vietnam

"castrati" (127): Italian opera singers whose high voices were the result of castration before puberty.

"Fu Manchu, Charlie Chan, Number One Son, Hop Sing" (127): All stereotyped Orientals in fiction and the movies – where they were frequently played by Occidental actors in heavy makeup.

"*Breakfast at Tiffany's*" (127): The movie *Breakfast at Tiffany's* (1961) starred Audrey Hepburn (1929-1993) as Holly Golightly, a free-spirited New York socialite and Mickey Rooney as I. Y. Yunioshi her Japanese landlord.

"Auteur" (127): A film director whose personal influence and artistic control over all aspects of production make the movie identifiably his/hers. Woody Allen is often cited as an example.

"mise-en-scène" (128): The arrangement of scenery and stage properties in a play.

"Ken doll" (128): Boyfriend of Barbie doll.

"*Hard Knocks … Venice Beach*" (128): There was a 1980 movie called *Hard Knocks* and a 1982 movie called *Venice Beach*, but neither film matches those described in the novel which they each post-date.

"Didion … Chandler … Faulkner … Welles" (128): Joan Didion (born 1934), American writer and journalist; Raymond Thornton Chandler (1888-1959), American-British novelist and screenwriter noted for detective fiction; William Cuthbert Faulkner (1897-1962), American writer and winner of the Nobel Prize; George Orson Welles (1915-1985), American actor and director/producer.

"Joseph Buttinger and Frances Fitzgerald" (130): Buttinger (1906-1992), expert on East Asia and author of numerous books on Vietnam; FitzGerald (born 1940), author of *Fire in the Lake: The Vietnamese and the Americans in Vietnam* (1972) which won the Pulitzer Prize and other awards.

"punji trap" (131): A booby trap comprising a spike or spikes of wood or bamboo sharpened and heated.

"Joseph Goebbels" (134): Paul Joseph Goebbels (1897-1945) was Reich Minister of Propaganda of Nazi Germany from 1933 to 1945.

"Milton's Satan" (134): In *Paradise Lost* (1667-1674), the epic poem by John Milton (1608–1674), Satan expresses the conviction that it is, "Better to reign in Hell than serve in Heaven."

"trompe l'oeil" (134): Literally meaning 'deceive or trick the eye,' this is a form of painting in which the representation of an object is so life-like that it appears to be real to the viewer.

Commentary

The narrator's meeting with the Auteur in his Hollywood Hills home is uncomfortable and raises more questions in his mind about his identity. His reaction to the script he has read is that it is full of stereotypes, most obviously that the South Vietnamese are "*humble, simple people*" (126) and the Viet Cong "battle-wizened men (and women) who had slaughtered Frenchmen" (125). Violet, the Auteur's personal assistant, treats him abruptly and he concludes that "the cause of her behavior was my race" (127). In America, white is an "all or nothing" thing, and he is "half an Asian" (127). Perhaps this is why, when he is talking about how the anti-communist Montagnards are portrayed in the film, he calls them "my people" and refers to "my country" (131). He is angry that the movie gives not a single line of intelligible dialogue to a Vietnamese character. Their arguments about how the Vietnamese scream is another example of absurd humor used for satirical effect.

The narrator comments bitterly that the war in Vietnam "was the first war where the losers would write history instead of the victors" (134). He describes Hollywood as "the most efficient propaganda machine ever created" which, in the case of this film, would deny the Vietnamese people a voice in their own history by showing "white men saving good yellow people from bad yellow people" (134).

The sympathizer's argument with the Auteur spills over into his talk with the General and Madam. When the General suggests that Sonny's reporting is too outspoken, the captain initially defends what the journalist has written. Very quickly, however, he puts back on the mask of his "character, the good captain" and supports the General's plan to remind Sonny "of how we do things back home"; that is, censorship of the media was maintained by beating the reporters and editors who stepped out of line (137). In return for having to say (and potentially do) things in which he does not believe, the narrator gains information on CIA-backed plans for the re-invasion of South Vietnam using Thailand as a staging post.

Chapter 9

18. Why does the narrator accept the offer of employment in the Philippines working as a consultant during the shooting of the movie *The Hamlet*?

19. What does he learn in the Philippines about the fate of the South Vietnamese who are living under the communist regime?

20. How would you describe his memories of his dead mother? Does he blame her or admire her for the way in which she brought him up?

Notes

"susurrus" (139): Soft and gentle whispering or murmuring.

"dialectical materialist" (141): Marx and Engels adapted the metaphysical insight that a higher level of existence emerges inevitably from and has its roots in the lower (as in the Theory of Evolution) to apply to human society which they saw as developing a classless society out of a class society.

"Ali Baba" (146): In the Arab folk tale *Ali Baba and the Forty Thieves*, Ali opens the magically blocked entrance to a cave containing fabulous treasure by saying the magic words, "Open sesame."

"*Fodor's Southeast Asia*" (147): One of a series of guides for travelers. Today (2018) the book is in its 23rd edition!

"*War and Peace*" (147): This 1869 novel, by Count Lyov (Lev) Nikolayevich Tolstoy (1828-1910), is one of the longest in any language. It deals with Napoleon's disastrous invasion of Russia in 1812.

"Bataan" (151): A province on the west side of the Philippine island of Luzon about 600 miles east of Vietnam.

"boat people" (151): Name given to over one million refugees who fled Vietnam, Cambodia and Laos by boat and ship following the victory of the North in 1975. This exodus was at its height 1978-1979, but continued through the early 1990s.

"*petit écolier*" (154): Biscuit topped with milk chocolate.

Commentary

The abrupt about-turn of the Auteur gets the narrator to the Philippines to prepare for the shooting of the movie. He justifies going on the basis that he will be "*undermining the enemy's propaganda*" (142), but another motive is his "Catholic chorus of guilt" over the murder of the major and his desire to "provide some support for the major's wife and children" (140). He identifies with the children because, like him, they are "innocents to whom wrong was done" – in this case by him (140). In the sympathizer's past his mixed blood caused his mother's family (particularly his aunts) to exclude him from the children's play and from the New Year gift-giving. In all of this, however, his memory of his dead mother is of her unconditional love and pride in him. To this injustice, he attributes his conversion to communism by Man, and now, ironically, his "aunt" is in Paris and is a conduit through which he sends secret information back to the communist government in Vietnam.

The description of setting up a front organization, the Benevolent Fraternity, and manipulating the Congressman to channel secret money into it is more openly political than anything so far in the novel. The narrator exposes just how politicians manipulate and how they are manipulated. In this case, the sympathizer, firmly in his role as the good captain, convinces the Congressman that money unofficially diverted to the cause of the Vietnam refugees will be converted into votes, while the Congressman knows that this money will be used "to engage in illegal activities" against the communist regime about which he can plausibly deny knowing anything.

In the Philippines, the sympathizer finds a miniature of the situation he has lived through in Vietnam: "Uncle Sam ... supporting the tyrant Marcos" against insurgencies by both the communists and the Muslims (149). From one of the extras he recruits, he learns that following the communist victory "the conditions in our homeland were as bad as rumored ... Our own people victimizing and terrorizing and humiliating us." His informant adds with bitter irony, "I suppose that's improvement" since the Vietnamese are no longer being "victimizing and terrorizing" by foreigners (152). Not surprisingly, on hearing this, the narrator's conscience is troubled, and his guilt about having killed the major returns.

The captain doubts the justification he had for accepting the job on the movie: he had gone in order to make more realistic the representation of Vietnamese people, but his lowly position means that he is virtually powerless to do that. He reflects, "I was little more, perhaps, than a collaborator, helping to exploit my fellow countrymen and refugees" (153). He finds some justification in turning one of the film-set graves into a monument to his beloved mother.

Chapter 10

21. There is a great deal of satire in the narrator's description of shooting the movie. Give three examples of his use of humor to mock the Auteur and those who work for him.
22. Nevertheless, his experience on the movie set stirs unpleasant memories and questions in the sympathizer. Give two examples where he is driven to question the actions of the communists whom he supports.

Notes
"Fellini" (157): Federico Fellini (1920-1993), famous and influential Italian film director and screen-writer.
"Sunset Strip" (157): Iconic stretch of road in West Hollywood, California.
"ARVN" (161): The Army of the Republic of Vietnam.
"Warhol painting" (163): Andy Warhol (1928-1987), American painter and filmmaker.
"savant" (163): A person (often a young person) with significant mental disabilities who demonstrates certain intellectual abilities far above the average.
"Sophia Loren" (166): Sofia Villani Scicolone (born 1934), a sultry Italian film actress and singer.

Commentary
The sympathizer is caught between two unacceptable opposites. The

capitalist West is represented by the film on which he is working. The party thrown for the Auteur is culturally insensitive (not to say plain racist) in its presentation of 'natives,' and the film is little better. There are now three speaking parts for Vietnamese in the film, but the parts are not played by Vietnamese actors because, Violet explains, none was suitable. He reflects, "What Violet was telling me was that we could not represent ourselves" (158). On the other hand, the communist East, represented by Vietnam, seems to be a place from which people want only to escape because of persecution. These people inevitably incite his sympathy and through Man's aunt he unwisely asks, *"Is this really happening? Or propaganda?"* (161). Perhaps it is questions like this that got him into prison. He asks the Commandant directly, "If our revolution served the people, why were some of these people voting by fleeing?" (161).

The sympathizer's inability to see just one side of the war is clear when he describes the absurd comedy of the Vietnamese extras not wanting to play the parts of Viet Cong. He writes, "Nobody wanted to be Viet Cong (i.e., the freedom fighters) ... The freedom fighters among the refugees despised these other freedom fighters with an unsettling, if not unsurprising, vehemence" (162). Only the captain would use the same idealistic term for both sets of combatants, suggesting as it does moral equivalence.

The description of the waterboarding of James Yoon's character, Binh, is complex. It is part comedy since none of the Vietnamese actors want to play Viet Cong (a difficulty that is solved by double pay) and the Vietnamese actors involved in the scene cannot make any sense of the Auteur's direction. It is also part paradox since the scene is fake (James Moon has a stunt double and the blood is artificial), but it takes on an intensity that is so real that it recalls to the captain's mind watching the torture of the female communist agent. He comments, "But that was real, so real I had to stop thinking about her face" (170).

Watching the filming, the sympathizer recalls that he was lectured on torture techniques by Claude in the National Interrogation Center. Significantly, he feels that the rape scene in the Auteur's movie is unnecessary, perhaps because it threatens to stir memories that are too painful. Inevitably, the sympathizer is forced to acknowledge that both sides used precisely the same inhuman methods, "a real prisoner's mortification continued for days, weeks, months, years. This was true of those captured by my communist comrades, according to our intelligence reports, but it was also true of those interrogated by my colleagues in the Special Branch" (168-169). To the narrator, no one is innocent; all are guilty, especially himself.

Chapter 11

23. Explain why the sympathizer feels that his work on the film has been a failure.
24. What draws him to the mock cemetery?

25. What suppressed memory does his white hospital room bring to the surface? Explain the final sentence of the chapter, "I was not a bastard, I was not a bastard, I was not, I was not, I was not, unless, somehow, I was" (193).

Notes

"Mao at Yan'an" (172): The Yan'an Forum on Literature and Art was held in May 1942. Mao Zedong's speeches were edited and published as *Talks at the Yan'an Forum on Literature and Art*. His thesis was that art must serve the advancement of socialism.

"Baudelaire" (173): Charles Pierre Baudelaire (1821-1867), French poet most famous for his controversial volume *Les Fleurs du Mal* (*The Flowers of Evil*, 1857) for which he, his publisher and printer were prosecuted for offense against public morals.

"Panzer division" (174): In World War II, the German Army used a tactic called blitzkrieg. This involved a rapid, coordinated strike by Panzer divisions comprising tanks, artillery and infantry with air support.

"F-5s" (175): Tactical fighter used extensively in Vietnam.

"B-52 Stratofortress" (178): A Boeing-produced jet bomber.

"Zsa Zsa Gabor" (184): (1917-2016), Hungarian-American actress who certainly had "va-va-va-voom" (i.e., the quality of being interesting, exciting, or sexually appealing).

"Hank Williams" (187): Hiram 'Hank' Williams (1923-1953), an American singer-songwriter on the Country Music genre.

"President Truman … Hiroshima" (187): President Truman ordered the atom bomb to be dropped on the Japanese city of Hiroshima on August 6th, 1945. This continues to be a controversial action.

"the secret zone of Binh Duong Province" (188): Bình Dương Province is located in the Southeast region of Vietnam, north of the city that was Saigon and is now Ho Chi Minh City. The secret zone was a Viet Cong safe zone.

"Z-99" (188): I could find no reference to the terrorist group Z-99.

Commentary

In his work on *The Hamlet*, the narrator increasingly sees himself as "not only a technical consultant on an artistic project, but an infiltrator into a work of propaganda" (172). His aim is to subvert the film's intention to present an exclusively American view of the Vietnam War. His role as a sleeper, or mole, is to work actively, in plain sight, for the cause. Man has convinced him that "the mole is the beauty spot on the nose of power itself" (174). Yet though he knows this, the sympathizer still regards himself as more like the "subterranean, worm-eating mammal … surely ugly to all except its own mother, and nearly blind" (174). He is fundamentally unhappy in the role he has been forced to play.

The description of the production is full of satirical humor from the extras who have to "die more than once, many four or five times," to the oxymoronic

35

command, *"Dead Vietnamese, take your places!"* (175), to the use of "white, uncooked sausages" to represent exposed intestines (176). The deaths of individual are also described as comic from the foul tasting fake blood, to the Thespian's unwashed stink that keeps people at least fifteen feet from him, to the ultimate "absurdity" of the Auteur's claim (which is not without some truth) that his film, being a "great work of art is … as real as reality itself, and sometimes even more real than the real" (178).

The sympathizer knows that the film will represent the war for those who see it in later generations; that it is "just a sequel to our war and a prequel to the next one that America was destined to wage" (179). He feels that he has failed because, though he has ensured some accuracy in the film, the film's fundamental ideology is false. Speaking of the power of America over nations like Vietnam, the captain writes, "They owned the means of productions, and therefore the means of representation, and the best we could ever hope for was to get a word in edgeways before our anonymous deaths" (179).

Things turn serious when the sympathizer learns that his beloved cemetery is to be blown up as part of the film's climax. This place serves as a real point of contact with his dead mother. However, the movie action begins while he is still there and he is badly injured by explosions. The extras who visit him in hospital tell him that the rumor is that the Auteur ordered the explosions to be started early in order to punish the sympathizer for his opposition to the director's ideas during the filming.

The white hospital room reminds the narrator of the white cell in the National Interrogation Center in Saigon where he was in charge of interrogating a Viet Cong bomb-maker. The man was driven to commit suicide, and it was the narrator who (responding angrily to the man's mocking of his muddled heritage) drove him to it by threatening to publicize a fake confession in which the man admitted to being gay. The captain admits to the Commandant that he did not fulfill his role as a mole (a sleeper agent for the communists). Instead, so annoyed was the captain by the prisoner's insult that he, "took pleasure in what I was supposed to do and not supposed to do, interrogate him until he broke, as Claude had requested" (192). The irony is that the narrator is writing his confession in an identical white cell where he "had nothing but time to ponder this event I had whitewashed from my mind" (191). The captain, a communist agent playing the role of an interrogator of communists, is now (it is increasingly clear) a lapsed communist being interrogated by real communists.

Chapter 12

26. What progress has the General made in organizing a communist resistance force in the captain's absence?

27. In what ways does the narrator find the clock in the shape of the homeland that had the time set for Saigon symbolic of the desire of the exiles to overthrow the communists (199)?

28. Explain the way in which the sympathizer's consciousness has been impacted by the concept of Original Sin.

Notes
"we had surrounded the Chinese in Cholon" (195): Cho Lon is a district of Saigon, now Ho Chi Minh City.
"femme fatale" (203): A beautiful, seductive woman in a novel or movie who will ultimately bring disaster to any man who becomes involved with her.
"Che Guevara" (211): Ernesto 'Che' Guevara (1928-1967), Marxist revolutionary and friend of Raúl and Fidel Castro whom he accompanied on their invasion of Cuba which deposed the American-backed dictator Fulgencio Batista in January 1959.
"postprandial" (210): The period after a meal – in this case dinner.

Commentary
"Not to own the means of production can lead to premature death, but not to own the means of representation is also a kind of death" (194). The narrator takes Marxism to another level. In the modern world, being defined by someone else is the same as not existing. This is what he feels has happened to the Vietnamese people in the movie *The Hamlet* despite his best efforts.

As he hears the General's plans for a military incursion into Vietnam, he knows that they are impractical and will fail. The clock, in the shape of Vietnam and set to display Saigon time, is to him a symbol that the refugees "were only going in circles" (199).

The sympathizer gives half of his compensation money ($5,000) to the major's widow to calm his conscience. He writes, "what is more revolutionary than helping one's enemy and his kin?" (204), but he knows that *he* is the one seeking forgiveness and that it is the ghost of the dead major that frightens him. We learn that he is obsessed by the doctrine of Original Sin: every man is doomed to commit "sins and crimes" – there are no innocent humans (209). This is another aspect of the sympathizer's inability to see any issue from just one side. [Later, he will remember his priest/father's teaching that "Since all were guilty of Original Sin, even punishment wrongly given was in some way just" (246).]

Chapter 13
29. The narrator attacks Sonny for being a socialist who "always talked … about how much [he] believed in the people and the revolution so much" but who stayed and still stays in California away from the struggle in Vietnam. Explain what effect the captain anticipated that his criticism would have and why it does not bring the result he anticipated.
30. What do you make of the sympathizer's enigmatic dream (226)?

Notes

"Simon de Beauvoir, Anaïs Nin, Angela Davis" (212): Simone Lucie Ernestine Marie Bertrand de Beauvoir (1908-1986), socialist French intellectual; Angela Anaïs Juana Antolina Rosa Edelmira Nin y Culmell (1903-1977), French writer and sexual liberationist; Angela Yvonne Davis (born 1944), black socialist American political activist and writer.

"Adam to Freud" (212): Adam is (presumably) the first man in *Genesis*; Sigismund Schlomo Freud (1856-1939) is the Austrian founder of psychoanalysis.

"anaphylactic" (212): Severe allergic reaction.

"Yellow Peril" (218): A slogan used throughout the Western World to describe the perceived threat posed by inferior Asians. Having initially encouraged Chinese migration to the U.S., in the late nineteenth and early twentieth centuries as a source of cheap labor, laws were passed to stop immigration from China.

"Ming the Merciless" (218): A character who first appeared in the Flash Gordon comic strip in 1934 and popularized by the movie serials of Flash Gordon in the 1930s.

"kapok tree" (226): A tree native to the rainforests which can grow up to 200 feet in height. "Due to its extreme height, the kapok, or ceiba tree, towers over the other rainforest vegetation. Some varieties of the ceiba tree are characterized by spines or conical thorns, giving the tree a menacing appearance" (Rainforest Alliance).

Commentary

This chapter returns to the predicament of Asians living in America, whether they are immigrants like Sonny and the captain or natural born citizens like Sophia. Sonny admits, "I learned, against my will … that it's impossible to live among foreign people and not become changed by them … I feel a little foreign to myself as a result" (216). The narrator tries to shame Sonny in Sophia's eyes by pointing out that, though he claims to support the socialist cause, he did not return to Vietnam to fight for the communists in the civil war after he finished college and has not returned now that the communists have taken over to play his part in rebuilding the country. Instead of arguing, Sonny agrees, "I admit that I am afraid. I admit my cowardice, my hypocrisy, my weakness, and my shame" (216). Sophia, however, recognizes that she too has the same weaknesses; she accepts her boss's patronizing view of her as an Oriental, so she empathizes with Sonny. The narrator knows that he has lost her to Sonny.

The sympathizer attends training with the General's army and forwards details to Paris. He knows that what is being planned is a suicide mission and knows why men are prepared to sacrifice themselves. The men whom the General has recruited join up because they have "been humbled by what they had been turned into here in exile" (219). They have lost status both within society and within their own families, but when they put on a uniform their "manhood" is "renewed" (219). The narrator comments:

> The General's men, by preparing themselves to invade our now
> communist homeland, were in fact turning themselves into new
> Americans. After all, nothing was more American than wielding a gun
> and committing oneself to die for freedom and independence, unless it
> was wielding that gun to take away someone else's freedom and
> independence. (218)

Here we can see that the captain has come to see the political/military slogan 'freedom and independence' to be entirely meaningless, since it is used to justify oppression in the name of liberation. Both the communists and the anti-communists claim to be 'revolutionaries' whose aim is "to liberate the people" but all that they really want is power over them (220).

Bon explains why he is willing to go on what is effectively a suicide mission. He tells the captain, "this world I'm living in [i.e., California without his wife and son] isn't worth dying for! If something is worth dying for, then you've got a reason to live" (224). He feels shame for having abandoned Vietnam, and effectively also his wife and his son since they died and he did not.

That night the sympathizer has an enigmatic nightmare. Perhaps it symbolizes his paranoia: as a spy he listens to what everyone says, but they are also listening to him waiting for his first false statement to uncover his true identity.

Chapter 14

31. Why does the General blame the captain for Sonny's article exposing the Fraternity and opposing its aims?
32. The sympathizer tells the story of his first meeting with Man and Bon and how the three became blood brothers. Then he comments, "A pragmatist, a true materialist, would dismiss this story and my attachment to it as romanticism" (233). What does the sympathizer's continuing loyalty to both Man and Bon show about his limitations as a communist sleeper agent?
33. There is a long description of how the narrator attempts to seduce Lana (apparently successfully). What plot developments might this open up?

Notes

"Mata Hari" (228): Margaretha Geertruida 'Margreet' MacLeod née Zelle (1876-1917), Dutch exotic dancer who was convicted and executed for spying for Germany during World War I.

"Pham Duy" (234): Pham Duy (1921-2013), Vietnamese singer and songwriter whose work was banned by the communists. After the fall of Saigon, he moved to California but returned to Vietnam in 2005, by which time restrictions on his music were being lifted.

"Camus" (234): Albert Camus (1913-1960), French intellectual and writer who wrote of the meaning to be found in a meaningless existence.

"Tay Ninh" (236): A provincial city in south-western Vietnam.

"Cher ... Nancy Sinatra" (237): Respectively: Cherilyn Sarkisian (born 1946), American singer and actress; Nancy Sandra Sinatra (born 1940), eldest daughter of Frank Sinatra, American singer and actress.

"*anh hoi*" (238): A generally used term of affection or endearment – like saying 'dear'.

"Ghandi, Martin Luther King Jr., and Thich Nhat Hanh" (242): Mohandas Karamchand Gandhi (1869-1948) used nonviolent civil disobedience in the 1940s against British rule to gain Indian independence. Martin Luther King Jr. (1929-1968) led nonviolent protests against segregation in the U.S.A in the 1950s and 1960s. Thich Nhat Hanh (born 1926) Vietnamese monk, Zen master, poet, and peace activist.

"Billie Holliday, Dusty Springfield, Elvis Phoung, and Khanh Ly" (242): Respectively: Eleanora Fagan (1915-1959), iconic American jazz singer; Mary Isobel Catherine Bernadette O'Brien (1939-1999), English pop singer; Pham Ngoc Phuong (born 1945), popular Vietnamese singer; Nguyen Le Mai (Mai Nguyen) (born 1945), Vietnamese singer born in Hanoi.

Commentary

Pressure builds on the narrator when the General sees an article by Sonny that exposes the Fraternity as a front organization for a planned military campaign to overthrow the communists in Vietnam. The General is unhappy with his intelligence officer, the captain, for not having warned him earlier of Sonny's communist sympathies. Ironically, he tells the narrator, "You're too sympathetic" (231). The General suggests, euphemistically, that something may need to be done about Sonny – just as something had been done about the major. The captain has no alternative but to agree; he is trapped in his role.

We learn how the narrator, Man and Bon became friends in childhood when Man and Bon stepped in to stop him being bullied because of his mixed race. This memory helps to explain why the sympathizer is not an effective communist. He confesses, "A pragmatist, a true materialist, would dismiss this story and my attachment to it as romanticism" (233). He has not forgotten the story, though his loyalties to Ban and to Man are politically incompatible.

Watching *Fantasia* in the Roosevelt Hotel, the narrator gets close to Lana. By the end of the night, he is sure he "would posses her and that she would have [him]" (243).

Chapter 15

34. What is the author's purpose in describing the discussion at the County Club meeting?

35. Give one example of satirical humor.

Notes

"Pham Duy, Trinh Cong Son ... Duc Huy" (245): Pham Duy (1921-2013),

Vietnamese singer/songwriter; Trinh Cong Son (1939-2001), famous Vietnamese artist, songwriter and musician; Duc Huy (born 1947), Vietnamese singer.

"aspsara" (245): Young and beautiful supernatural woman.

"Marcos and Suharto" (257): Ferdinand Emmanuel Edralin Marcos Sr. (1917-1989), President of the Philippines from 1965 to 1986. In reality, he was a brutal and corrupt dictator. Suharto (1921-2008), President of Indonesia from 1967 to 1998. His rule was authoritarian and corrupt, though he was popular during the 1970s and 1980s.

"Dr. Mengele" (261): Josef Mengele (1911-1979), German SS officer and physician in Auschwitz concentration camp where he performed cruel and often fatal 'medical' experiments on prisoners.

Commentary

The captain feels himself to be in the General's power because of his failure to reveal Sonny's socialist leanings. He is troubled by the 'ghost' of the major he had killed (a product of his conscience) and desperately wants to be free of his image. He remembers writing to Man about his father after his mother's death, *"How I wish he were dead!"* (249). What does not appear to occur to the captain at this point is that writing this to Man was very much the same as the General telling him that something needed to be done about Sonny: effectively, he was asking Man to have his father killed, whether he was aware of having done so or not. He records that his father "died not long after" without appearing to connect the two things.

The main point of the satirical account of the meeting at the Country Club is to expose the thinking of the U.S. strategists on the threat of communism. In this chapter, the narrative is definitely slanted against the Americans who seem to have no real understanding of either happiness or liberty. They are interested only in retaining American influence around the globe and, in order to do this, they are prepared to support tyrants such as "Marcos and Suharto" (257).

The chapter's final joke is that the "Country Club" turns out to be a high-end brothel. The joke is in the pun on *"Count*ry." Compare: "HAMLET to Ophelia: Lady, shall I lie in your lap? OPHELIA: No, my lord. HAMLET: I mean, my head upon your lap? OPHELIA: Ay, my lord. HAMLET: Do you think I meant *country* matters? OPHELIA: I think nothing, my lord. HAMLET: That's a fair thought to lie between maids' legs." (*Hamlet* 3.1.)

Chapter 16

36. Explain why the narrator insists on shooting Sonny himself.
37. What reasons almost prevent him from doing the deed?

Notes

"palimpsest" (264): A manuscript on which the original writing has been erased to allow it to be written over and thus reused.

"chiaroscuro" (264): An effect of contrasted light and shadow in art.

"hydroponic" (266): Growing plants in sand, gravel, or liquid, with added nutrients but without soil.

"Walther P22" (271): A semi-automatic pistol described by the makers as "a stylish, fun gun to own."

"Monet" (272): Oscar-Claude Monet (1840-1926), French artist and leading exponent of Impressionist painting.

"Khmer Rouge" (273): The Khmer Rouge was the military arm of the Communist Party of Kampuchea, led by the Marxist dictator, Pol Pot, which ruled Cambodia between 1975 and 1979, during which period almost two million people were slaughtered.

Commentary

The captain now finds himself trapped. His desire to return to Vietnam with the General's forces in order to try to save Bon's life makes him vulnerable to the General's condition that he can only go on the mission if he kills Sonny. On the other hand, Man writes secretly ordering him to stay in America because that is where he is most valuable to the communist cause.

Bon, who has killed many times during the war, reassures the narrator about killing Sonny, "If it makes you feel any better, this isn't murder. It's not even killing. It's assassination" (267). It occurs to the captain that Sonny may well be a communist agent like himself, or that the General and Madam might be the communists. One just does not know who is on what side. He recalls Man telling him, "You'll be surprised who gets the medals after the liberation" (268).

The shooting of Sonny has been meticulously planned by Bon, who has also offered to do the necessary killing, but the narrator insists on performing the act himself. At the last minute he loses his nerve and tells Sonny that he is an under-cover communist agent. The captain is making a desperate attempt to connect with someone who knows who he actually is. Even as a child, he wore the mark of "bastard" and was judged by people on his appearance, and now he is tired of wearing the mask that a spy must wear. He writes, "I cannot be the only one who believes that if others saw who I really was, then I would be understood and, perhaps, loved" (275). Sonny, however, does not believe him and suspects a trap. Sonny's anger seals his fate, though the sympathizer nearly botches the shooting. Ironically, he puts on a disguise so that he looks like "just another unremarkable white man" before making his escape (278).

Chapter 17

38. Compare and contrast the reactions of the sympathizer and of Bon to watching the movie *The Hamlet*.

39. What do we learn of the reason why the General changed his mind about allowing the captain to go to Thailand?

Notes

"Hmong" (283): The U.S. Central Intelligence Agency (C.I.A.) recruited the

Hmong people in Laos to fight against the North Vietnamese Army. In the late 1970s large numbers were evacuated as refugees.

"KUBARK" (284): A C.I.A. manual of interrogation techniques, including torture.

"M16" (291): American-made automatic rifle.

Commentary

Together Bon and the narrator watch *The Hamlet* in a movie theater in Bangkok. Despite himself, the sympathizer finds he is caught up in the emotion of the film and has to admit that the Auteur made an effective film. His name, however, does not appear in the credits, leading the narrator to comment angrily, "Failing to do away with me in real life, he had succeeded in murdering me in faction, obliterating me utterly in a way that I was becoming more and more acquainted with" (289). Once again, his identity has been denied.

Bon's verdict on the film is harsh. He tells his friend, "You tried to play their game, okay? But they run the game. You don't run anything. That means you can't change anything. Not from the inside. When you got nothing, you got to change things from the outside" (289). The captain writes sadly, "I had failed at the one task both Man and the General could agree on, the subversion of the Movie [sic] and all it represented, namely our misrepresentation" (289-290).

On leaving California, the sympathizer learned that the General only let him go because he had heard that the captain tried to seduce his daughter Lana. (He appears not to know that the two spent a night together.) The General says, "How could you ever believe we would allow our daughter to be with someone of your kind? … You are a fine young man, but you are, in case you have not noticed, a bastard" (291). The narrator can say nothing to this word – a word that has been used against him all of his life. Once again, his identity has been denied.

In the forest, the sympathizer and his friends meet what Claude calls, "The last men standing of the armed forces of the Republic of Vietnam" (292). These men look nothing like elite Rangers; in fact, they resemble Viet Cong. They also meet the admiral (who bears a striking resemblance to Ho Chi Minh). It thus seems that roles in Vietnam have reversed, but nothing has actually changed – one ideology is the same as another. Bon has lost all faith in ideology. He tells the admiral, "I used to believe, but not anymore … I just want to kill communists. That's why I'm the man you want" (294).

Chapter 18

40. Look at the description of the explosion that kills the lieutenant. Do you find any comedy in the way the incident and its aftermath are presented?

40. Why does Bon cry when he and the narrator are captured?

Notes

"Mekong Delta" (294): The delta of the Mekong River in southwestern Vietnam to the west of Ho Chi Minh City (Saigon).

"M79" (295): A shoulder-fired grenade launcher.

"PRC-25 radio" (296): The standard American portable field radio during the Vietnam War.

"Nihilism" (296): A philosophy that asserts that life is meaningless and that no religious or moral values have any claim to authenticity so that one action is equivalent to another action.

"Radio Free Vietnam" (296): The anti-communist group radio network of the self-styled Government of Free Vietnam. It is located in Southern California and still broadcasts to Asia.

"James Taylor and Donna Summer" (297): James Vernon Taylor (born 1948), best-selling American singer-songwriter; LaDonna Adrian Gaines (1948-2012), American singer-songwriter at the height of her popularity in the late 1970s.

"julienned" (298): Food cut into short, thin strips.

"cajeputs" (298): A form of tree native to South Asia.

"Quang Ngai" (303): Quang Ngai is a city in central Vietnam. This incident may be based on the infamous My Lai Massacre of 1968 when up to 500 unarmed people were massacred by U.S. Army soldiers.

"arroyo" (303): A dry gulch that fills with flood water after heavy rain.

"lianas" (304): Woody plants that climb the trunks of trees in tropical forests.

Commentary

The group's first sortie into the jungle is their last. The lieutenant steps on a mine and his legs are blown off. The grizzled captain smothers the screaming man because he has no chance of survival. There is some black comedy in the description of retrieving the lieutenant's body parts, "the gunner said, Where's his leg? … Where's the foot? said the dark marine" (302). As they bury the dead lieutenant, the captain again is troubled by hallucinations of the dead major and Sonny.

Later the same day, as they are trying to cross the river, the patrol is ambushed and only Bon, the narrator, and five others survive – Bon who wanted to die and the narrator who, at the height of the firefight, realized that he "feared death and loved life … yearned to live long enough to smoke one more cigarette, drink one more drink…" (307). Bon cries telling his friend, "If it wasn't for you, you stupid bastard … I'd die here" (307).

Chapter 19

41. Explain the communist concept of "reeducation."

42. Is there anything that the Commandant says to the narrator that makes you reevaluate the conflict between the communists of the North and the anti-communists of the South? (The baby in the bottle, for example.)

43. The Commissar turns out to be Man. Did you see that coming? Why? or Why not?

Notes

"the unexamined life is not worth living" (311): A famous statement attributed by Plato to Socrates at his trial for impiety and corrupting the youth of Athens. He was found guilty and sentenced to death.

"Red Guards" (312): A militant movement in China whose members were totally dedicated to furthering Mao's Cultural Revolution (1966–76).

"*How the Steel Was Tempered* or *Tracks in the Snowy Forest*" (312): Respectively, a 1936 socialist realist novel set during the Russian Civil War (1918–1921) by Russian novelist Nikolai Ostrovsky (1904–1936), and the 1957 novel about an elite band of soldiers fighting brigands in the mountains by Chinese novelist Qu Bo (1923–2002).

"To Huu" (312): Vietnam's most popular revolutionary poet (1920-2002) whose works were largely written between 1937 and 1946. He rose to be deputy prime minister but was dismissed in 1985 following failed economic policies that resulted in hyper-inflation.

"Nguyen Du" (314): Nguyen Du (1765-1820), Vietnamese poet.

Commentary

The sympathizer's confession is finally finished, though the camp Commandant declares himself far from satisfied with it. The narrator has spent "a year in an isolation cell from which [he] was allowed to emerge only an hour a day for exercise" (309). The Commandant insists that he is not a prisoner but he is also not a guest since he is not free to leave. He is rather a patient undergoing reeducation.

The Commandant tells the narrator that, given his dual ethnicity (his destiny of being a bastard), "You would be better off if you only saw things from one side. The only cure for being a bastard is to take a side" (314). This is effectively what people have been telling him to do all of his life. He replies that "the only thing harder than knowing the right thing to do … is to actually do the right thing" (314).

The chapter allows the author to give voice to the communist view of the revolution. To the Commandant the suffering of the prisoners is nothing compared to the suffering of the communists in their fight with the Americans. To him, the revolution can do no wrong because it is ultimately for the greatest good of the people.

The meeting with the Commissar is a surprise because he turns out to be Man, horribly disfigured in combat. This explains the Commandant's comment, "*He* sees much more potential in you than I do" (322).

Chapter 20

44. Why is Man treating the sympathizer as he is? What are Man's aims for the interrogation?

45. What is it that the narrator has to tell Man to make this treatment end?

Notes

"Phan Ban Chau" (337): Phan Boi Chau (1867-1940), early political advocate for the independence of Vietnam.

Commentary

The interrogation brings to mind O'Brien's interrogation of Winston Smith in Orwell's *1984*. There Smith must say that he loves Big Brother, but he must not only say it, he must also *feel* it to be true.

We learn that Man, hideously disfigured (ironically by bombs dropped by a South Vietnamese 'plane defending Saigon), sought assignment in this camp knowing that the captain and Bon would be brought there if they were captured. He assures the captain that he is there to save the lives of his two friends, but that to do so he must convince the Commandant and his superior commissars that they have been successfully reeducated.

Man reminds the narrator that he once wrote to him about something he forgot but could not remember what it was (330). Readers will see this as a reference to the captain's 'accident' on the film set after which in his confession he wrote, "I had forgotten something, but what that something was I did not know … I've lost a piece of my mind … A portion of my memory … completely erased" (202). It is this memory that the captain must recover before he can be released, Man tells him.

In this case, Man wants to know what the narrator did to the "'communist agent with the papier-mâché evidence of her espionage crammed into her mouth'" (336). He reminds the captain that "You mentioned her four times in your confession … but we don't learn her fate. You must tell us what you did to her" (336). Evidently the captain is repressing this memory; all he can reply is that he did not do anything to her.

It is difficult to grasp what Man wants. Is it only for the captain to confess something that will satisfy the Commandant or is it something more? What does Man mean when he tells his old friend, "Only without the comfort of sleep will you fully understand the horrors of history" (337)? And why should a communist speak of the "horrors of history" when Marxism sees history as a process toward a classless society? Why is the answer "Nothing" not quite the right answer to the question, "What is more precious than independence and freedom?" (331)? It is perhaps appropriate that the reader shares the narrator's own confusion about these questions at this point in the narrative.

Chapter 21

46. What does the narrator remember about what happened to the "'communist agent with the papier-mâché evidence of her espionage crammed into her mouth'" (336)? Why do you think that he has repressed this memory?

Notes

"Ben Tre" (341): This might refer back to in January and February of 1960 when

46

the Viet Cong occupied Ben Tre Province and began instituting communist land reforms. Although the South Vietnamese Army (ARVN) eventually recaptured the province, spontaneous uprisings spread to other regions of South Vietnam effectively beginning the civil war. It might equally be another battle in this region.

"kanji" (347): Chinese characters used in the Japanese system of writing.

Commentary

Ironically, the interrogation techniques used by Man are ones that the captain himself has seen used on Viet Cong suspects. Man tells him that "Everything being done to you comes from" the book *KUBARK Counterintelligence Interrogation, 1963* that was found in the captain's quarters in the General's villa (344).

Under interrogation, the narrator *does* remember what happened to the woman who had been arrested with the names of communist agents – a memory that he has presumably repressed because it is so horrible. Despite his efforts to prevent it, the woman was raped by three guards and he had to just sit and watch. This rape is an ironic parallel of the rape of the innocent villager by four Viet Cong in *The Hamlet*.

Chapter 22

47. What further admission comes from the narrator during his interrogation?
48. Explain why Man puts his gun into the narrator's hand and points it at his own forehead.
49. The chapter ends with the narrator's thought, "I was, at last, enlightened" (368). Explain what you understand him to mean by this.

Notes

"Tokarev" (361): A Russian semi-automatic pistol.
"doula" (367): A woman trained or experienced to assist during childbirth – a midwife.
"frenulum" (367): A fold of skin beneath the tongue, or between the lip and the gum.

Commentary

The Commandant's accusation against the captain is that he was not willing to "sacrifice" himself "to save the [female] agent, though she was willing to sacrifice her life to save the commissar's [i.e., Man's]" (356). The sympathizer now understands that he "was not being punished or reeducated for the things I had done, but for the things I had not done" (256-257).

The save his friend's life, Man gets the captain to admit to another crime: that he effectively killed his father. The narrator now remembers that he "had written to Man … *I wish he were dead*" (358). Of course, his first impulse is to claim that in doing so he had not meant for Man to have his father killed, but

Man quickly corrects him, "Of course you did! Who did you think you were writing to?" (358). Finally, the narrator accepts that he wanted his father dead.

The sympathizer admits wanting to die because he has always been a man divided between two identities in a world "where hardly anyone accepted me for who I was, but only ever bullied me into choosing between my two sides" because, "This was not simply hard to do – no, it was truly impossible, for how could I choose me against myself?" (361). The man who could only be a sympathizer simply wants to end his own suffering. Then Man puts a pistol in his hand but points the barrel at his own forehead. Man wants to die not because of his hideous disfigurement but because he has lost all faith in the cause for which he was prepared to murder and torture. He has realized the absurdity that the communists reeducate those who are already "too educated" – people who have the capacity to judge for themselves (363). Under the communists, "All the jargon that the cadres spout only hides an awful truth – ... Now that we are the powerful, we don't need the French or the Americans to fuck us over. We can fuck ourselves just fine" (364). Man's position has become untenable because he is supposed to teach something in which he no longer believes. It seems that the narrator wants to die because he has found that death is the thing "more precious than independence and freedom" – the two supposed goals of the revolution (360) – while Man has realized that the revolution has not solved Vietnam's problems.

Under further torture (the continuous sound of a baby screaming), the sympathizer finally understands the answer that is required of him, "It was me, screaming the one word that had dangled before me since the question was first asked – nothing – the answer I could neither see nor hear until now – nothing! – the answer I screamed again and again and again – nothing! Because I was, at last, enlightened" (368). The answer that Man wants from the captain is the answer he has himself come to: there is no ideology which can give transcendent meaning to life – not Catholicism, not capitalism, and not communism. Life has no meaning – this is the only basis of understanding upon which life can be lived.

Chapter 23

50. On page 376, the narrator begins to refer to himself in the first person plural ('we' replaces 'I'). Explain why he does this.
51. The narrator concludes on a hopeful note. On what does the narrator base his belief in life? What kind of revolution is he still in search of?

Notes

"Molotova truck" (377): A truck produced in the Soviet Union.

Commentary

The narrator tells us that the political Commandant "saw only one meaning in nothing – the negative, the absence, as in *there's nothing there*," or on the slogan (used equally by communists and anti-communists) that 'nothing is more precious than independence and freedom' (371). What the narrator has understood is "the *positive* meaning ... the paradoxical fact that nothing is, indeed, something" (371).

Man is also a divided man, just like the captain: he is "the Commissar but ... also Man; ... my interrogator but also my confidant; ... the fiend who had tortured me but also my friend" (374). The narrator now understood that "the true optical illusion was in seeing others and oneself as individuals and whole, as if being in focus was more real than being out of focus" (374). This is the error that ideology makes.

Man has arranged for the sympathizer and Bon to escape from Vietnam. Ironically, he has done so through bribery. Using the Commissar's share of the money that desperate women have given to the guards in order to visit their prisoner husbands, Man bribes the police to look the other way as the narrator and Bon make their escape from the country. Man says, "Isn't it remarkable that in a communist country money can still buy you anything you want?" The sympathizer responds, "It's not remarkable ... It's funny" – a statement which goes a long way to explain the absurd humor of much of his written confession (375). The truth that he has "understood, at last, how our revolution had gone from being the vanguard of political change to the rearguard hoarding power ... Having liberated ourselves in the name of independence and freedom – I was so tired of saying these words! – we then deprived our defeated brethren of the same" (376). 'Freedom' and 'independence' are meaningless terms, but 'nothing' is not meaningless: it is the fundamental truth about human life. He is convinced that a terrible joke has been played on those who fought on both sides of the conflict: millions have died for absolutely nothing – that is the joke.

Saigon appears to be a sullen, joyless place. The only music allowed is revolutionary music. Vietnam has invaded Cambodia and China has invaded Vietnam. Communism has proved to be yet another God that has failed. And so it goes... – as Kurt Vonnegut repeatedly writes in his novel *Slaughterhouse Five*.

The ending of the book is an affirmation of the value of life. The sympathizer knows that those who are escaping with him and Bon will "in turn turn our backs on the unwanted, human nature being what it is"; nevertheless, he insists, "we are not cynical. Despite it all – yes, despite everything, in the face of nothing – we still consider ourselves revolutionary. We remain the most hopeful of creatures, a revolutionary in search of a revolution..." (382).

The narrator has faced the harsh truth of nothingness – the emptiness of life and the illusion of all of its values. However, he has reacted not by seeking self-destruction but by seeing life itself as a value, "*We will live!*" (382). This seems identical to the analysis of the human condition by Albert Camus (who is mentioned on page 234 of the narrator's confession):

> I see many people die because they judge that life is not worth living. I
> see others paradoxically getting killed for the ideas or illusions that

give them a reason for living (what is called a reason for living is also an excellent reason for dying). I therefore conclude that the meaning of life is the most urgent of questions ... In certain situations, replying "nothing" when asked what one is thinking about may be pretense in a man. Those who are loved are well aware of this. But if that reply is sincere, if it symbolizes that odd state of soul in which the void becomes eloquent, in which the chain of daily gestures is broken, in which the heart vainly seeks the link that will connect it again, then it is as it were the first sign of absurdity. (*The Myth of Sisyphus*, 1942)

It is important to understand that for Camus, recognition of the absurdity of life (which he defined as becoming aware of the inevitable conflict between the human desire to find transcendent meaning in life and life's refusal to provide any basis for such transcendent meaning) is the only reasonable basis on which to live one's life. Lacking the transcendent values of religion and political ideology, life itself becomes a value because it is the only thing that we *know* we have.

Retrospective questions

These questions take a more holistic view of the text. They are designed for group discussion, though they might prove equally useful as aids to individual reflection on the novel or even to written responses.

1. In his essay "Our Vietnam War Never Ended," Nguyen writes, "most Americans don't understand how many of the immigrants and refugees in the United States have fled wars – many of which this country has had a hand in" (389). This statement contains two separate assertions, both highly controversial. Examine your reaction to both assertions. To what extent does the novel validate the author's point? (Note that in the penultimate paragraph of the essay, Nguyen gives specific examples.)

2. In his essay/Interview "Anger in the Asian American Novel," Paul Tran defines the novel as a portrayal of "the individual in the wake of failed revolutions" (393). What revolutions fail in the novel and what does their failure leave the individual (including the reader) clinging onto?

3. Nguyen says that, in the novel, he "wanted to be very critical of the role of the Americans in Vietnam" but that he also "didn't want to let anybody off the hook, so the book is also very critical of South Vietnamese culture and politics and Vietnamese communism" (395). Did you find the novel to be as even-handed as the author claims? Do you think that it is actually possible (or even desirable) to write a novel, on this or any other topic, that is completely even-handed?

4. Nguyen says, "There's not really a solution that the book offers at the end, because for me the adventures – or misadventures – of our narrator haven't been completed yet" (401). Do you consider that a sequel would be either desirable or possible? Provide a brief outline of such a sequel.

5. Nguyen says, "I want this book to provoke people to rethink their assumptions about this history, and also about the literature they've encountered before – to make them uncomfortable in a good way" (403). Did the novel make you feel uncomfortable? About what? With what effect?

6. Comparisons have been made between *The Sympathizer* and Joseph Heller's satirical war novel *Catch-22*. One such example of absurdist, black humor is the captain's heavily ironic statement, "It was a smashingly successful cease-fire, for in the last two years only 150,000 soldiers had died. Imagine how many would have died without a truce!" What other examples of satiric comedy come to mind? How does the inclusion of black humor affect your feelings about the novel?

7. The narrator says that the war in Vietnam "was the first war where the losers would write history instead of the victors." Has reading the novel changed your understanding and appreciation of the movies, documentaries and novels about

the Vietnam War that you have seen?

8. Talk about the novel's conclusion. Does the novel have an optimistic ending? If so, on what is that optimism based.

Suggestion for Further Reading

The Quiet American (1955) by Graham Greene
This novel, set in Vietnam in the 1950s, was remarkably accurate in predicting the end of French colonialism and the growth of American involvement in Vietnam. It also foresaw the disastrous consequences of American involvement.

Where Have You Gone, Charming Billy? (1975) and *The Things They Carried* (1990) by Tim O'Brien
The former is a single short story and the latter a collection of linked, semi-autobiographical short stories. Both draw on O'Brien's own experiences in Vietnam where he served from 1969 to 1970. O'Brien has written an number of other books. All are worth reading.

Catch-22 (1961) by Joseph Heller
This classic anti-war satire is set in Italy during the Second World War. It exploits the absurdity of war in a number of nightmare, almost surreal situations. It may be, as one published said in rejecting the novel, the same joke over and over again, but it is a very good joke.

Structure

The novel deals with a sequence of distinct episodes:
- The fall and evacuation of Saigon;
- The relocation of Vietnamese evacuees in Guam;
- The resettlement of these evacuees in California;
- The formation of a military republican resistance movement;
- The writing and shooting of the movie *The Hamlet*;
- The planning, preparation and mounting of an armed patrol into Vietnam;
- The capture and interrogation of the narrator who is one of several survivors of the patrol;
- The narrator's second escape from Vietnam.

Although most of these episodes feature the same small group of characters, it is only the presence of the narrator that holds *all* of them together. Any one of the episodes might have been a sufficient basis for a novel, and it is a valid question whether, taken together, they form a coherent and consistent whole, particularly since the tone of the writing varies between episodes. For example, the most uniformly comic and satirical is the episode about the filming of *The Hamlet*, an episode that appears essentially unconnected to the main plot as though the author forced it into a story which would have lost nothing had it not been included. On the other hand, it could be argued that satirical humor is present in all of the episodes and that each of them illustrates the basic themes of the novel.

Narrative Voice

The author has said that he "took about three months ... all of summer 2011" writing and rewriting that first six sentences of the novel until he felt that they were just right because he "knew that the entire novel would be driven by the voice of this narrator because it's all from his perspective" (Charley Rose Interview). The entire novel is written in first person from the perspective of the sympathizer: Chapters 1 to 18 are the confession that he writes for the Commandant during his first year of solitary confinement in prison; Chapters 19 to 23 are a continuation of this confession, written for the narrator's own benefit, which he begins after his interrogation by Man has concluded and which must have been finished following his escape from Vietnam.

The narrator has no privileged insight into the feelings or thoughts of the other characters in the novel. In fact, he turns out to be a poor judge of character on occasions. For example, he is shocked that Sophia begins an affair with Sonny while he is away in the Philippines because he has not understood her liberated attitude to sex. Again, the narrator is confident that the General is the one person who does not care, or even notice, that he is of mixed race, but he is disillusioned

54

when the General calls him a bastard with whom he would never let his daughter have a relationship.

The narrator frequently expounds on his own thoughts and experiences, but he is no more reliable in what he says about himself than in what he says about others. His narrative is a process by which he *comes to understand* himself by releasing repressed memories which enables him to see himself honestly for the first time. For example, it is only during his interrogation by Man that he realizes that he really *did* want his father to die, that he effectively told Man to have him killed – a request that Man acted upon. Similarly, for most of the narrative he regards himself as someone innocent of killing (Sonny is the first person he has actually killed) and torturing because in Vietnam he was merely an administrator, an on-looker. A key aim of Man's interrogation of the captain is to make him realize the degree of his own guilt for the deaths and pain of others (most notably the rape of the female communist agent).

Two features of the style of the writing are relevant here: the author's decision not to use speech marks in the passages of dialogue and to use long paragraphs throughout. The result is that *The Sympathizer* is neither simple nor straightforward reading. It has been suggested that the author's aim is "that the text flows on and on and comes to resemble stream-of-consciousness" because:

> The author is not attempting neat, ordered clarity – instead, this device effectively creates the sense that many voices are concentrated in one: that our narrator is in an endless monologue with himself, weighing first one position, then the next; and that the other characters are versions of himself, united by humanity but divided by belief systems. (Jai Arjun Singh, "Book Review," Scroll.in)

A third feature of the style is described by Dana Dumitru:

> the language sounds archaic (or maybe extremely correctly by the British canon), with weird phrasings ("but although I forgot not a word", "but I was bothered not in the least", "This was the prayer many a general and politician said", etc.) and a lot of words of French descent (lycée, coup d'état, sorties, évacuées, cinema-marquee, valise, dames, entendre). ("*The Sympathizer*", Bookish Style)

These linguistic features perfectly fir the narrator's background since English is not his first language and French is probably his second language.

Settings

The novel begins and ends in Vietnam. At the start of the novel, it is April, 1975. American forces having pulled out two years earlier, the army of the Republic of [South] Vietnam is disintegrating and the communist forces of the Democratic Republic of [North] Vietnam are closing in on Saigon (which would fall on April 30th). The country is war-torn and increasingly in chaos. The Americans attempt to coordinate the evacuation of their own citizens and those Vietnamese who have worked for them whom the communists will treat as traitors and collaborators. The entire operation is, however, a shambles in which many are killed and many left behind. Whilst he is filming in the Philippines, the narrator hears troubling stories of brutal repression by the communists and of hundreds of thousands fleeing the country in boats that are hardly sea-worthy. At the close of the novel, after the narrator has returned to Vietnam with troops sent by the General to attempt to reinvade the country, he discovers that things are no better under the communists. The prisons are the same; the interrogation methods are taken from the C.I.A. handbook; the government has invaded Cambodia and been invaded by China so the war goes on; and bribery is just as rife as it ever was. The people have not been liberated; they have simply got new masters.

The Vietnam refugees are first taken to Guam where they are placed in over-crowded camps in which conditions are degrading. When they are flown to California, they are again placed in camps, though these are not so crowded and have more amenities. Gradually, the refugees leave the camps and begin their new lives in California. The anti-war feeling of a few years ago has largely dissipated, but the immigrants are not particularly welcome and the Vietnamese tend to stick together in their own communities. The men feel the change the most. They, who were once soldiers, no longer have a function; many of them have to take jobs that they consider menial and beneath them. The married women, who at home in Vietnam never went out of the home, now find that they have to work because the family needs the money, though for some this is a liberating experience (Madam, for example, proves to be an excellent cook and opens a restaurant). The children adapt to American culture much more quickly than their parents, and this causes conflict within the family.

The captain travels to the Philippines to shoot the movie *The Hamlet* and, with bitter irony, comments that "I felt at home the instant I stepped from the air-conditioned chamber of the airplane … I was again in a country with its neck under a dictator's loafer … [The] state of martial law was underwritten once more by Uncle Sam … all in all, the Philippines made a nice substitute for Vietnam itself…" (148-149). Through his narrator, the author is making the point that, following the Truman Doctrine, the U.S.A. will support any dictator, no matter how brutal or corrupt, who promises to offer stability in the face of communist or Muslim revolutions.

Most of the action in the Philippines revolves around the film set. Ironically, the crew has built "a complete reproduction of a Central Highlands hamlet down to the outhouse mounted on a platform above a fishpond" (150). It is just such a village as that where the captain was born and spent his childhood, though he feels no nostalgia for the primitive nature of life there having experienced the comforts of America – the author extracts a great deal of comedy from the captain's description of the open-air toilet perched over the fishpond and his reluctance to use it. The only thing lacking is people, but even these are soon brought in, and thanks to the captain, they are actually Vietnamese people. The irony, of course, is that nothing is real and that it is all going to be blown up for the climax of the movie, so the film set becomes a metaphor for American involvement in Vietnam and other countries.

Genre

> "The hooks of the novel, though, are definitely the thriller and 'Vietnam War novel' genres" ("Book Club Redux: 'The Sympathizer'").

Historical Novel

The term historical fiction (or the historical novel) applies to works set in a period at least twenty-five years (some definitions extend that to fifty years) before their composition (e.g., a work such as James Fennimore Cooper's *The Last of the Mohicans* which is set in 1757 and was written in 1826). Another definition states that the action must take place before the author could personally have experience the events related. Based on both of these definitions, *The Sympathizer* is right on the cusp. It was first published in 2015, exactly forty years after the fall of Saigon. The author was born on March 13th, 1971, in Ban Me Thuot in the Central Highlands of what was then South Vietnam, but his family took him to the U.S.A. when he was four. This means that he could not have directly experienced the events he writes about in the novel, though he clearly draws on his family history as well as on more formal research.

Historical fiction by definition includes historical people and actual events; it usually also includes fictional characters and imagined events. Artistic license is permitted in regard to the presentation and interpretation of both characters and events, so long as the author does not deviate in significant ways from the established facts of history. One criterion by which a historical novel may be judged is the skill with which the author blends the real and the imagined. In *The Sympathizer* real people are kept in the background; they are largely the political leaders of the countries in which the novel is set. Their place is taken by what I will call 'generic historical figures' such as the General, the Commandant, the Commissar and the Congressmen. These people are not individualized with names because they are archetypes, representative of real people and drawn with a keen eye to historical accuracy. The narrator is also unnamed and he too represents a very real historical type. Nguyen told NPR:

> there really were spies in South Vietnam that rose to the very highest ranks of the South Vietnamese bureaucracy and military. And there was a very famous spy named Pham Xuan An who was so important that, during his time as a mole, he was promoted to a major general by the North Vietnamese. And he was friends with people like David Halberstam and all the important American journalists. And they had no idea that he was a communist spy who had studied in the United States. ("Author Interview," National Public Radio)

A key question that may be asked of any historical novel concerns the *use* that the author makes of the received history on which the novel is based. The most common criticism of historical novels is that they tend (in the tradition of

58

Sir Walter Scott) to romanticize the past. That fault is certainly not evident in *The Sympathizer* where the sense of time and place is often rendered with absolute and excruciating realism (though it is only fair to add that in other places the past is presented as absurd comedy). There is no doubt that the author has a political agenda, for while it is true that no individuals or groups are presented as admirable or even blameless, the weight of Nguyen's criticism falls on America because, as his narrator sees it, the Americans made promises to the people of South Vietnam that they broke – effectively the U.S.A. used South Vietnam to slow the spread of communism in the Far East and then just walked away from the mess they had made.

Bildungsroman (The Coming of Age Novel)

A Bildungsroman tells the story (often, but not always, in the first person) of the growing to maturity of a young, intelligent, and sensitive person who goes in search of answers to life's questions (including the biggest question of all: who they actually are) by gaining experience of the adult world from which they have before been protected by their youth. The story tells of the protagonist's experiences in the world and of the inner, psychological process of his/her growth and development as a human being. (Examples would include *Jane Eyre* by Charlotte Bronte, *The Portrait of the Artist as a Young Man* by James Joyce and *Sons and Lovers* by D. H. Lawrence.)

This obviously applies to the development of the protagonist of *The Sympathizer*, despite the fact that (being presumably in his mid-twenties at the start of the action) he is a little older than is normal. The entire novel is about the narrator's education, his growth to self-knowledge, and indeed the text is the medium through which he discovers himself.

Here, by way of comparison, is what Amory Blain, the protagonist of F. Scott Fitzgerald's novel *This Side of Paradise* (1920), has learned by the end of the novel:

> Life opened up in one of its amazing bursts of radiance and Amory suddenly and permanently rejected an old epigram that had been playing listlessly in his mind: "Very few things matter and nothing matters very much." … Here was a new generation, shouting the old cries, learning the old creeds, through a revery of long days and nights; destined finally to go out into that dirty gray turmoil to follow love and pride; a new generation dedicated more than the last to the fear of poverty and the worship of success; grown up to find all Gods dead, all wars fought, all faiths in man shaken.... (Bk. 2 Ch. 5)

There are obvious parallels between this conclusion and the final pages of *The Sympathizer* because the protagonist of a coming of age novel goes forward to encounter life with a wisdom that he/she did not previously have. That wisdom has been gained through trial and suffering – though not normally through the brutal 'enhanced interrogation techniques' used on the captain.

Spy Thriller

Nguyen has said, "As for the thriller, I like plots, and this genre offers the opportunity to deploy strong plotting with crime, violence, and sex, all things I like in my fiction. I didn't get as much sex in as I wanted. Or drugs. Those have to wait for the sequel" ("Book Club Redux: 'The Sympathizer'").

The thriller sections of the novel are those that take place in California. The captain is a John le Carré-style double agent, a man ostensibly working for the anti-communist republicans while being in reality a communist spy. As for a strong plot there are two murders, secret meetings, and dark money filtered through front organizations. Nevertheless, it is difficult to see the novel as a thriller: it is a work that draws on many genres – perhaps too many for it to be really consistent and coherent.

Satire

Much of the novel is very funny but in a disturbing way. The narrator finds war absurd rather in the manner of Joseph Heller in *Catch 22* (1961). If you have read that book, you will recall the episode in which First Lieutenant Milo Minderbinder, the mess officer at the U.S. Army Air Corps base, contracts with the Germans to use American planes to bomb his own base because doing that is more efficient for the Germans and very profitable for Milo. This episode neatly symbolizes the insanity of the entire war. In *The Sympathizer* there is plenty of corruption (though not on the same scale), but the corruption under the communists is exactly the same as the corruption under the republicans which makes all of the killing pointless. The evacuation of Saigon is a farce (literally): the deejay cannot find the recording that is the secret signal for evacuation; everyone in Saigon knows what the secret signal will be; the rooftops of buildings one which helicopters are to land have been pained by Vietnamese women who have passed the information to the Viet Cong; and with typical insensitivity the Americans have named the evacuation "Frequent Wind," a name suggestive of flatulence so that "all the bad air whipped up by the American helicopters was the equivalent of a massive blast of gas in the faces of those left behind" (85). There are many other examples of black comedy, such as the problems the soldiers have finding all of the body parts of a man who has stepped on a mine.

The most sustained satire comes in the episode describing the captain's involvement with the script and the filming of *The Hamlet*. Nguyen has said, "I wanted to get my revenge on *Apocalypse Now*. Satirizing the moviemaking allowed me both to have fun with the movie … The effect is hopefully tragicomic … in satirizing the racial and national attitudes that underlay both the filmmaking and the warmaking on the part of Americans (and to show them as connected)" ("Book Club Redux: 'The Sympathizer'"). The scene where the narrator demonstrates to the director different kinds of screams is almost surreal;

the description of the Thespian (obviously a method actor) who does not wash for three months, with the predictable result that no one can get anywhere hear him, is comic exaggeration; and then there is the absurd dispute over the Vietnamese extras refusing to play Viet Cong parts until they are offered double pay. The episode certainly achieves Nguyen's stated aims.

Other targets seem less effective. In the same interview Nguyen states, "I had some fun with academic satire with a couple of the professorial characters." He is referring to Professor Avery Wright Hammer and the Chair of the Oriental Studies Department. The former is gently mocked for his oddities but the latter is harshly satirized because he really understands virtually nothing about Orientals but insists on pontification about their beliefs and values.

The Picaresque Novel

This is a fictional narrative that follows the adventures of a young hero (or, less commonly, heroine) who wanders through life (often on a journey). The structure of a picaresque novel is thus episodic. Picaresque novels normally have a realistic style that is often combined with elements of comedy and satire, which defines the style of *The Sympathizer* precisely. While the captain is not the lovable rogue typical of the genre, he *is* low-born (which is another common feature of the genre) and he does go on a journey in which he visits four different countries without always being in control of the direction he has to take. Henry Fielding's *The History of Tom Jones, a Foundling* (1749) and Mark Twain's *Adventures of Huckleberry Finn* (1884) each contain significant elements of this genre.

Prison Literature

This genre is characterized by a narrative written while the author or the narrator is confined against his will. It may be fiction or non-fiction. Self-evidently *The Sympathizer* fits this genre since it is composed of two confessions written largely during the narrator's time as a captive in a communist reeducation prison. E. E. Cummings's autobiographical novel *The Enormous Room* (1922) was written while he was imprisoned by the French during World War I accused of anti-war sentiments, and Arthur Koestler's (1940) *Darkness at Noon* tells the story of Rubashov, a Bolshevik who is arrested, imprisoned, and tried for treason against the Soviet Union. Often prison literature involves extended periods of interrogation, and this is true of *The Sympathizer*. Readers will find it interesting to compare the interrogation of the captain with O'Brien's interrogation of Winston Smith in George Orwell's *1984* (1949).

Themes

Seeing Issues from Both Sides

Nguyen explains that the novel explores "what it means to be able to not only sympathize with the people we love and we care for but to sympathize with our enemies…" He elaborates:

> As a young boy growing up, I was both American and Vietnamese, and I was completely split in two by the experience of watching [*Apocalypse Now!*] … As an American … I see it through American eyes, I'm rooting for the American soldiers, and then they kill Vietnamese people. At that moment I think, am I American, or am I Vietnamese? Am I the one I'm supposed to identify with or am I the one being killed, and that dilemma has driven me partly to write *The Sympathizer*. (Charley Rose Interview)

From the very start of the novel, the narrator establishes that, despite his allegiance to the communist cause, he always sees both sides of every question and that this tendency is related to his mixed heritage as a Eurasian. Thus, he identifies with the soldiers defending Saigon; they are as much his countrymen as are the Viet Cong attacking the city. In the context of the war, he finds himself unique: every other character is convinced of the righteousness of the cause for which he/she fights, is willing to inflict any degree of suffering on the enemy, and (in most, though not all, cases) is personally prepared to make any sacrifice, including death.

Unsurprisingly, the novel is supportive of the viewpoint of the sympathizer and exposes the inhumanity of the committed. This is illustrated in the character of Man who is the only character in the novel that changes radically. Initially, it is he who converts the captain to communism; it is he who is the teacher of dialectical materialism and the captain who is the student. However, Man comes to see that the communist revolution does not change the lives of the people of Vietnam, except in so far as it makes their existence worse, so again he becomes the narrator's teacher. This time his aim is to make the captain see that his uncommitted position is dishonest, while warning him that following any religious or political ideology is equally dishonest and disastrous. The narrator learns this lesson well. This is why he asserts on the final page "Despite it all – yes, despite everything, in the face of *nothing* – we still consider ourselves revolutionary" (382). What the narrator means by this is not explained.

In my opinion, the narrator's position is close to that of Albert Camus's conception of human revolt against the human condition as expressed in his novel *The Plague* (1947) and his collection of philosophical essays *The Rebel* (1951). In the latter, Camus writes:

> Metaphysical rebellion is the movement by which man protests against his condition and against the whole of creation. It is metaphysical because it contests the ends of man and of creation. The slave protests

against the condition in which he finds himself within his state of slavery; the metaphysical rebel protests against the condition in which he finds himself as a man. The rebel slave affirms that there is something in him that will not tolerate the manner in which his master treats him; the metaphysical rebel declares that he is frustrated by the universe. For both of them, it is not only a question of pure and simple negation. In both cases, in fact, we find a value judgment in the name of which the rebel refuses to approve the condition in which he finds himself.

Camus's position led to a break with those left-wing intellectuals (e.g., John Paul Sartre) who remained committed to the Soviet Union and were willing to ignore the mounting evidence tyranny and repression. However, though Camus could no longer support the socialist revolution, he remained a rebel determined to improve the human condition. That is a clear description of the philosophical position of the narrator at the end of the novel.

Memory

Two aspects of memory are explored in the novel: individual memory and group memory. Of the former, Nguyen has said, "The novel is very much about memory, both of the coerced kind (the narrator is being strongly encouraged to remember) and the uncoerced kind (he very much wants to remember certain things and people)" ("Book Club Redux: 'The Sympathizer'"). The captain can never forget his first meeting with Bon and Man who came to his aid when he was being beaten by bullies. This memory, he admits, makes him a romantic rather than a communist revolutionary. Similarly, he has very warm memories of his mother because she was the person who taught him to sympathize with others, which is also at odds with his allegiance to communism. Then, there are the repressed memories that Man sets about bringing back into the captain's consciousness. These are things that he has done that he cannot acknowledge because they are so terrible. Until he does do so, however, he will never truly know himself.

Group memory in this novel means the different memories of the war that the republicans, the communists and the Americans have. In his novel *1984* (1949), George Orwell writes, "He who controls the past controls the future. He who controls the present controls the past." The victors in the war, the communists, write the history of the conflict, but their propaganda reaches only the people of Vietnam. The defeated Americans, however, control world-wide media (Hollywood movies and book publishing being the two most obvious examples), and so they are able to shape the history of the war not only for themselves but for most of the rest of the world. The republican Vietnamese, however, have no voice: their story has been lost, which is, of course, one of the reasons why Nguyen wrote this novel. He has said:

Well, we like to think that our memories are all equal, sort of a democratic notion, but in actuality, I think certain groups' memories dominate over other groups, and those are the groups that have control over the industries of memory ... Hollywood is one example of that, publishing is another ... That is why even though the United States lost the war in Vietnam, it won the war in memory because it controls these kinds of industries ... The Vietnamese could win in their country, [but] they can't win globally ... when people think about the Vietnam war, they think about how Hollywood has remembered it ... the industry of memory means that the U.S. – the military power of the U.S., is matched by its power to make movies. Vietnam can't make movies like 'Apocalypse Now' ... (Charley Rose Interview).

Betrayal and Loyalty

These two principles are in conflict throughout the novel. The life of a spy is, by definition, a life filled with betrayal since loyalty to the cause must win out over personal loyalties, friendships and even love. The narrator is the General's trusted aide-de-camp who lives in the same villa and eats at the same table as the General's wife and children, yet all the time he is spying on the General and reporting military information back to the Viet Cong through Man. In California, he continues to spy on the General's efforts to form an armed insurgency, and in doing so betrays and murders two people who are essentially innocent – the major, who is not a spy, and Sonny, who is a journalist doing the job that journalists do in the U.S.A. (but were not allowed to do in South Vietnam).

Both the narrator and Man keep their identity as communist agents secret from their best friend, Bon. While their personal loyalties allow the captain and Man to secure Bon's escape from Saigon, they agree to tell Bon that Man will be following them to America because they know Bon will not go otherwise. When, however, the captain is faced with the choice between returning to Vietnam with Bon in order to try to keep him alive and Man's direct order that he must stay in California, for the first time, the narrator chooses personal loyalty over ideological loyalty.

The communist agents are, however, only the most obvious of those who betray others. To return to the General, unlike his men, he does not stay in Saigon and fight to the last: he uses his political connections in the C.I.A. to get himself and his family out. Not only that, but he tells everyone (in Vietnam, Guam and California) that he will return to defeat the communists which is, at best, self-delusion. The humiliating way in which he is treated by the refugees in the camp on Guam shows how the ordinary Vietnamese people think about leaders like him. Then again, the General deceives the captain about his feeling for him. He gives the impression that he regards the captain almost as a son and that his mixed ethnicity is not a factor in the way he regards him. However, the moment the captain shows an interest in dating the General's daughter he reveals that he regards the narrator as a bastard and would never allow Lana to associate with him.

Finally, Man also betrays the communist ideology because he feels that following the victory in the war the communists have betrayed the people. He uses his position in the camp to reeducate his friend the narrator not as a communist (though he must give the Commandant the impression that this is what he is doing) but as a human being. He takes a considerable risk in getting the captain and Bon released from prison and in bribing the police to allow them to slip out of the country.

Duality

The first thing that the narrator tells the reader is that he is "a man with two faces ... [and] also a man of two minds" (1). Bear in mind that this is written *before* his reeducation by the commissar (Man), so he remains conflicted about his essential nature, unclear whether to call his duality "a talent ... [or] a hazard" (1). Initially, he links it only with his role as a spy, but it soon becomes clear that his divided psyche has a deeper origin in his parentage and nurture, and a still deeper origin in the history of his country. The narrator is the product of rape, the son of a French-Catholic priest who seduced child a poor Vietnamese girl aged thirteen. As a result, he is both a "bastard" and a Eurasion. The theme of two-facedness will run through this book: the narrator is a captain in the army of the Republic and a spy for the North; he is raised in Vietnam and educated in the U.S.A.; he is a committed communist spy and feels sympathy and admiration for those who fight for the Republic; he is a Vietnamese who (at the end of the novel) can never return to Vietnam. He is a man who does not know who he is but is surrounded by people who single-mindedly *do* know who they are; he is a man who belongs nowhere.

Vietnam itself is a nation whose people are divided between the North and the South; the people of the South are further divided between their own Vietnamese culture and the influence of Americanization. The narrator explicitly links the duality he experiences with that of his generation:

> No, just as my abused generation was divided before birth, so was I divided on birth, delivered into a postpartum world where hardly anyone accepted me for who I was, but only ever bullied me into choosing between my two sides. This was not simply hard to do no, it was truly impossible, for how I choose me against myself?

As he writes, the only proposed 'solution' to his dilemma (and by extension to the dilemma of the nation) is to choose one side and reject the other. This is the pressure he feels throughout the novel: the General demands loyalty to the Republic, and extracts from him the vow, "I am with you, sir ... To the end" (87); Man demands loyalty to the revolution, "secrecy and hierarchy were key to revolution, Man told me ... "independence and freedom" ... were words we were willing to die for" (27); the Chair of Oriental studies tells him, "You must assiduously cultivate those reflexes that Americans have learned innately, in order to counter weight your Oriental instincts" (65); Sophia tells him "I damn well know my culture, which is American, and my language, which is English" (76). Unfortunately, for the narrator such a choice is not possible; it does not represent a solution to his dualities because they are who he is.

Hope

The novel ends on an optimistic note. This is possible because the narrator has discovered a solution to his dualities: he has learned to embrace them. Nguyen has explained:

> It was deliberate for me to have my narrator, even as he has suffered tremendous disillusionment with communism and revolution, to insist that the response is not only to turn back to the individual but to acknowledge the importance of solidarity as well (hence the "we" of the end). ("Book Club Redux: 'The Sympathizer'")

Man, like the captain, was also a character with two faces: loyal Republican soldier and communist spy. However, having been terribly injured by napalm, he becomes the man with no face. This symbolizes that, ironically at the very moment of communist victory, his duality is erased not by the victory of one over the other but by the eradication of *both*, which liberates his own self. The narrator explains the effect of this liberation on Man, "The only benefit from his condition was that he could see what others could not, or what they have seen and disavowed, for when he looked into the mirror and saw the void he understood the meaning of nothing" (375). Man, having been a loyal communist, can now see *two* meanings in the slogan "nothing is more precious than independence and freedom" where before he had seen only one; he has also become "a man of two minds" (376). This is what he is able to teach the narrator through a process of reeducation.

The narrator's epiphany comes when he accepts his duality by saying, "I was that man of two minds, me and myself" (376). From this point on, the narrator refers to himself using the first person plural, "Everyone *we* met had wanted to drive *us* apart from each other, wanted *us* to choose either one thing or another, except the commissar" (emphasis added, 376). Never again in the novel will the narrator refer to himself as "I"; even more significantly, he identifies himself with the other refugees, "Collectively we will be called the boat people" (382). Secure now in his own identity, the narrator can move to the next stage which is solidarity with others – hence the incredibly powerful ambiguity of the final assertion, *"We will live!"* (382).

Symbols

The two-headed baby

Toward the end of his interrogation by the commandant, he shows the narrator "a greenish monstrosity ... [a] pickled baby with one body but two heads ... Two faces pointed in different directions" (315). The commandant states that he keeps the baby, a victim of chemical warfare waged by the Americans, preserved in formaldehyde to remind himself that, in the name of rebuilding the country, "Absolute honesty isn't always appreciated" (315). In other words, despite the fact that the communists have won the war, the struggle for communism continues and it still justifies double standards, lies and brutality. For the reader, the baby symbolizes the dualities described in the novel. It represents the divisions between North and South, and between Vietnam and the America. It also symbolizes the hypocrisy within the competing ideologies of the two sides, and the disastrous impact of colonialism (first French and then American) on the country of Vietnam. Finally, it symbolizes the narrator himself, since he was a man born with two minds who has been as a result a man with two faces for most of his life.

The gigantic insect

While living in California with Bon, the two are frequently drunk. On one occasion, the captain wakes from an intoxicated sleep in his La-Z-Boy recliner to be "frightened by the severed head of a gigantic insect gaping its jaws at me, until I realized it was only the wood-paneled television, its twin antennae drooping" (67). [This is surely a deliberate borrowing from the Edgar Allan Poe short story "The Sphinx" (1846).] Almost immediately, "The national anthem blared as the Stars and Stripes waved and blended with sweeping shots of majestic purple mountains and soaring jet fighters" (67). This comic incident has a serious side. The insect represents the monstrous force of American culture, broadcasting its version of events, exercising its controlling narrative, and drowning out the capacity of the Vietnamese to represent themselves.

The Rucksack

The narrator receives a rucksack with a false bottom when he graduates from college ironically from Claude, the C.I.A. agent. It symbolizes the captain's double-life as a spy. Ironically, he uses the false bottom to hide the "Minox mini-camera" which Man has given him (14). When he returns to Vietnam, he still carries the rucksack, but this time the false bottom contains his copy of Richard Hedd's *Asian Communism and the Oriental Mode of Destruction*, the code-book that he uses to communicate with Man (298). Finally, as the novel comes to a close, the narrator carries in the rucksack *both* Hedd's book and the manuscript of his confessions. Significantly, however, there is no mention of the false bottom at all (376-377). Like the narrator, the rucksack has become whole.

The Color Red

The narrator describes the first New Year celebration he can recall. Traditionally, the children receive red envelopes containing "lucky money" from each of their aunts and uncles, but the narrator received no envelope (and no apology) from Aunt Two (141). The others do give him envelopes, but his money is only half that of his cousins, one of whom explains, "That's because you're half-blooded" (141). The incident inflicts "scars" on the narrator's psyche and makes him open to Man's communist ideology (140).

For Man, the red envelopes symbolize "all that's wrong … primitive beliefs" that deny man control of his own destiny (141). In their place, Man states that "Red is revolution" (142). For Man, and for his convert the narrator (at that time), the difference is clear, but for the reader the symbolism actually links religion and communism. In the novel, communism will turn out to be "The God That Failed" (to quote the title of a book, published in 1949, of testimonies by ex-communist intellectuals).

Ghosts

Being Vietnamese, the narrator believes in ghosts and feels himself to be haunted by the undead spirits of the two men he murders the crapulent major and Sonny. They represent the guilt and shame he feels about having killed these two innocent men.

Literary Terms

NOTE: Not every one of these terms will be equally relevant to this particular text.

Ambiguous, ambiguity: when a statement is unclear in meaning – ambiguity may be deliberate or accidental.

Analogy: a comparison which treats two things as identical in one or more specified ways.

Antagonist: a character or force opposing the protagonist.

Antithesis: the complete opposite of something.

Climax: the conflict to which the action has been building since the start of the play or story.

Colloquialism: the casual, informal mainly spoken language of ordinary people – often called "slang."

Connotation: the ideas, feelings and associations generated by a word or phrase.

Dark comedy: comedy which has a serious implication – comedy that deals with subjects not usually treated humorously (e.g., death).

Dialogue: a conversation between two or more people in direct speech.

Diction: the writer's choice of words in order to create a particular effect.

Equivocation: saying something which is capable of two interpretations with the intention of misrepresenting the truth.

Euphemism: a polite word for an ugly truth – for example, a person is said to be sleeping when they are actually dead.

Fallacy: a misconception resulting from incorrect reasoning.

First person: first person singular is "I" and plural is "we".

Foreshadowing: a statement or action which gives the reader a hint of what is likely to happen later in the narrative.

Genre: the type of literature into which a particular text falls (e.g. drama, poetry, novel).

Image, imagery: figurative language such as simile, metaphor, personification etc., or a description which conjures up a particularly vivid picture.

Imply, implication: when the text suggests to the reader a meaning which it does not actually state.

Infer, inference: the reader's act of going beyond what is stated in the text to draw conclusions.

Irony, ironic: a form of humor which undercuts the apparent meaning of a statement:

> *Conscious irony*: irony used deliberately by a writer or character;
>
> *Unconscious irony*: a statement or action which has significance for the reader of which the character is unaware;
>
> *Dramatic irony*: when an action has an important significance that is obvious to the reader but not to one or more of the characters;
>
> *Tragic irony*: when a character says (or does) something which will have a serious, even fatal, consequence for him/ her. The audience is aware of the error, but the character is not;
>
> *Verbal irony*: the conscious use of particular words which are appropriate to what is being said.

Juxtaposition: literally putting two things side by side for purposes of comparison and/ or contrast.

Literal: the surface level of meaning that a statement has.

Melodramatic: action and/or dialogue that is inflated or extravagant – frequently used for comic effect.

Metaphor, metaphorical: the description of one thing by direct comparison with another (e.g. the coal-black night). Extended metaphor: a comparison which is developed at length.

Mood: the feelings and emotions contained in and/ or produced by a work of art (text, painting, music, etc.).

Motif: a frequently repeated idea, image or situation in a text.

Motivation: why a character acts as he/she does – in modern literature motivation is seen as psychological.

Narrator: the voice that the reader hears in the text – not to be confused with the author.

Oxymoron: the juxtaposition of two terms normally thought of as opposite (e.g. the silent scream).

Paradox, paradoxical: a statement or situation which appears self-contradictory and therefore absurd.

Pathos: is pity, or rather the ability of a text to make the audience or reader feel pity.

Perspective: point of view from which a story, or an incident within a story, is told.

Personified, personification: a simile or metaphor in which an inanimate object or abstract idea is described by comparison with a human.

Plot: a chain of events linked by cause and effect.

Protagonist: the character who initiates the action and is most likely to have the sympathy of the audience.

Realism: a text that describes the action in a way that appears to reflect life.

Rhetoric: any use of language designed to make the expression of ideas more effective (e.g. repetition, imagery, alliteration, etc.).

Sarcasm: stronger than irony – it involves a deliberate attack on a person or idea with the intention of mocking.

Setting: the environment in which the narrative (or part of the narrative) takes place.

Simile: a description of one thing by explicit comparison with another (e.g. my love is like a red, red rose).

     Extended simile: a comparison which is developed at length.

Style: the way in which a writer chooses to express him/ herself. Style is a vital aspect of meaning since how something is expressed can crucially affect what is being written or spoken.

Suspense: the building of tension in the reader.

Symbol, symbolic, symbolism, symbolize: a physical object which comes to represent an abstract idea (e.g. the sun may symbolize life).

Themes: important concepts, beliefs and ideas explored and presented in a text.

Third person: third person singular is "he/ she/ it" and plural is "they" – authors often write novels in the third person.

Tone: literally the sound of a text – How words sound (either in the mouth of an actor or the head of a reader) can crucially affect meaning.

Tragic: King Richard III and Macbeth are both murderous tyrants, yet only Macbeth is a tragic figure. Why? Because Macbeth has the potential to be great, recognizes the error he has made and all that he has lost in making it, and dies bravely in a way that seems to accept the justice of the punishment.

Literary Terms Activity

As you use each term in the study guide, fill in the definition of the term and include an example from the text to show how it is used. The first definition is supplied. Find an example in the text to complete it.

Term	Definition
	Example
Ambiguous, ambiguity	*when a statement is unclear in meaning- ambiguity may be deliberate or accidental*
Authorial comment	
Dialogue	
Diction	
Foreshadowing	
Image/imagery	

Term	Definition
	Example
Infer/inference	
Irony/ironic	
Dramatic irony	
Metaphor/ metaphorical	
Extended metaphor	
Motivation/ motive	
Narrative Voice	

Term	Definition
	Example
Symbolism	

Graphic Organizers

Plot

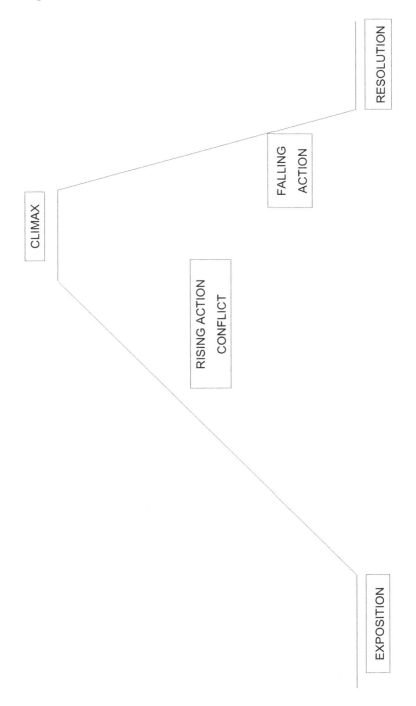

Different perspectives on the situation which initiates the action in the novel

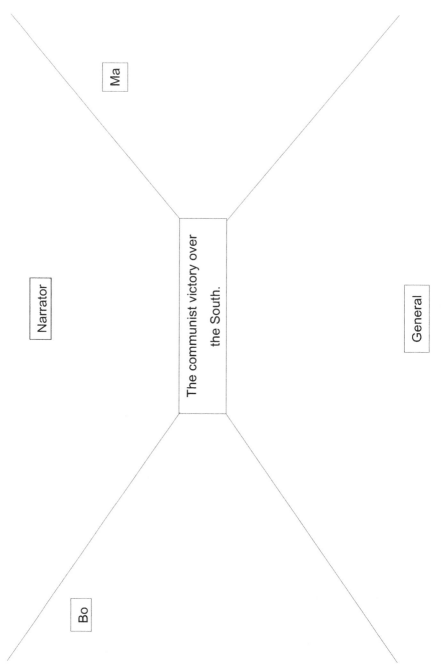

Ma

Narrator

The communist victory over the South.

General

Bo

Reading Group Use of the Study Guide Questions

Although there are both closed and open questions in the Study Guide, very few of them have simple, right or wrong answers. They are designed to encourage in-depth discussion, disagreement, and (eventually) consensus. Above all, they aim to encourage readers to go to the text to support their conclusions and interpretations.

I am not so arrogant as to presume to tell readers how they should use this resource. I used it in the following ways, each of which ensured that group members were well prepared for group discussion and presentations.

1. Set a reading assignment for the group and tell everyone to be aware that the questions will be the focus of whole group discussion at the next meeting.

2. Set a reading assignment for the group and allocate particular questions to sections of the group (e.g. if there are four questions, divide the group into four sections, etc.).
In the meeting, form discussion groups containing one person who has prepared each question and allow time for feedback within the groups.
Have feedback to the whole the on each question by picking a group at random to present their answers and to follow up with a group discussion.

3. Set a reading assignment for the group, but do not allocate questions.
In the meeting, divide readers into groups and allocate to each group one of the questions related to the reading assignment, the answer to which they will have to present formally to the meeting.
Allow time for discussion and preparation.

4. Set a reading assignment for the group, but do not allocate questions.
In the meeting, divide readers into groups and allocate to each group one of the questions related to the reading assignment.
Allow time for discussion and preparation.
Now reconfigure the groups so that each group contains at least one person who has prepared each question and allow time for feedback within the groups.

5. Before starting to read the text, allocate specific questions to individuals or pairs. (It is best not to allocate all questions to allow for other approaches and variety. One in three questions or one in four seems about right.) Tell readers that they will be leading the group discussion on their question. They will need to start with a brief presentation of the issues and then conduct a question and answer session. After this, they will be expected to present a brief review of the discussion.

6. Having finished the text, arrange the meeting into groups of 3, 4 or 5. Tell each group to select as many questions from the Study Guide as there are members of the group.

Each individual is responsible for drafting out an answer to one question, and each answer should be substantial.

Each group as a whole is then responsible for discussing, editing and suggesting improvements to each answer.

To the Reader

Ray Moore was born in Nottingham, England. He obtained his Master's Degree in Literature from Lancaster University and taught in secondary education for twenty-eight years before relocating to Florida with his wife. There he taught English at a Florida High School. He is now a full-time writer and fitness fanatic.

Website: http://www.raymooreauthor.com

Ray strives to make his texts the best that they can be. If you have any comments or question about this book please contact the author through his email: villageswriter@gmail.com

Also by Ray Moore:

All books are available from amazon.com and from barnesandnoble.com as paperbacks and at most online eBook retailers.

Fiction:

The Lyle Thorne Mysteries: each book features five tales from the Golden Age of Detection:

Investigations of The Reverend Lyle Thorne
Further Investigations of The Reverend Lyle Thorne
Early Investigations of Lyle Thorne
Sanditon Investigations of The Reverend Lyle Thorne
Final Investigations of The Reverend Lyle Thorne
Lost Investigations of The Reverend Lyle Thorne
Official Investigations of Lyle Thorne

Non-fiction:

The **Critical Introduction** series is written for high school teachers and students and for college undergraduates. Each volume gives an in-depth analysis of a key text:

"The General Prologue" by Geoffrey Chaucer: A Critical Introduction
"The Great Gatsby" by F. Scott Fitzgerald: A Critical Introduction
"Pride and Prejudice" by Jane Austen: A Critical Introduction
"The Stranger" by Albert Camus: A Critical Introduction (Revised Second Edition)

The **Text and Critical Introduction** series differs from the Critical introduction series as these books contain the original text and in the case of the medieval texts an interlinear translation to aid the understanding of the text. The commentary allows the reader to develop a deeper understanding of the text and themes within the text.

"Sir Gawain and the Green Knight": Text and Critical Introduction
"Jane Austen: The Complete Juvenilia": Text and Critical Introduction
"The General Prologue" by Geoffrey Chaucer: Text and Critical Introduction
"Heart of Darkness" by Joseph Conrad: Text and Critical Introduction

"Henry V" by William Shakespeare: Text and Critical Introduction
"Oedipus Rex" by Sophocles: Text and Critical Introduction
"A Room with a View" By E.M. Forster: Text and Critical Introduction
"The Sign of Four" by Sir Arthur Conan Doyle Text and Critical Introduction
"The Wife of Bath's Prologue and Tale" by Geoffrey Chaucer: Text and Critical Introduction

Study guides available in print - listed alphabetically by author
* denotes also available as an eBook

"ME and EARL and the Dying GIRL" by Jesse Andrews: A Study Guide
Study Guide to "The Handmaid's Tale" by Margaret Atwood*
"Pride and Prejudice" by Jane Austen: A Study Guide
"Moloka'i" by Alan Brennert: A Study Guide
"Wuthering Heights" by Emily Brontë: A Study Guide *
"Jane Eyre" by Charlotte Brontë: A Study Guide *
"The Stranger" by Albert Camus: A Study Guide
"The Myth of Sisyphus" and "The Stranger" by Albert Camus: Two Study Guides *
Study guide to "Death Comes to the Archbishop" by Willa Cather
"The Awakening" by Kate Chopin: A Study Guide
Study Guide to Seven Short Stories by Kate Chopin
Study Guide to "Ready Player One" by Ernest Cline
Study Guide to "Disgrace" by J. M. Coetzee
"The Meursault Investigation" by Kamel Daoud: A Study Guide
Study Guide on "Great Expectations" by Charles Dickens*
"The Sign of Four" by Sir Arthur Conan Doyle: A Study Guide *
"The Wasteland, Prufrock and Poems" by T.S. Eliot: A Study Guide
Study Guide on "Birdsong" by Sebastian Faulks*
"The Great Gatsby" by F. Scott Fitzgerald: A Study Guide
"A Room with a View" by E. M. Forster: A Study Guide
"Looking for Alaska" by John Green: A Study Guide
"Paper Towns" by John Green: A Study Guide
"Catch-22" by Joseph Heller: A Study Guide *
"Unbroken" by Laura Hillenbrand: A Study Guide
"The Kite Runner" by Khaled Hosseini: A Study Guide
"A Thousand Splendid Suns" by Khaled Hosseini: A Study Guide
"The Secret Life of Bees" by Sue Monk Kidd: A Study Guide
Study Guide on "The Invention of Wings" by Sue Monk Kidd
"Go Set a Watchman" by Harper Lee: A Study Guide
"On the Road" by Jack Keruoac: A Study Guide
"Life of Pi" by Yann Martel: A Study Guide *
Study Guide to "Death of a Salesman" by Arthur Miller

Study Guide to "The Bluest Eye" by Toni Morrison
"Animal Farm" by George Orwell: A Study Guide
Study Guide on "Nineteen Eighty-Four" by George Orwell
*Study Guide to "Selected Poems" and Additional Poems by Sylvia Plath**
"An Inspector Calls" by J.B. Priestley: A Study Guide
Study Guide on "Cross Creek" by Marjorie Kinnan Rawlings
"Esperanza Rising" by Pam Munoz Ryan: A Study Guide
"The Catcher in the Rye" by J.D. Salinger: A Study Guide
"Where'd You Go, Bernadette" by Maria Semple: A Study Guide
"Henry V" by William Shakespeare: A Study Guide
*Study Guide on "Macbeth" by William Shakespeare **
*"Othello" by William Shakespeare: A Study Guide **
"Oedipus Rex" by Sophocles: A Study Guide
"Cannery Row" by John Steinbeck: A Study Guide
"East of Eden" by John Steinbeck: A Study Guide
"The Grapes of Wrath" by John Steinbeck: A Study Guide
*"Of Mice and Men" by John Steinbeck: A Study Guide**
*"Antigone" by Sophocles: A Study Guide **
"Oedipus Rex" by Sophocles: A Study Guide
"The Goldfinch" by Donna Tartt: A Study Guide
"Walden; or, Life in the Woods" by Henry David Thoreau: A Study Guide
Study Guide to "Cat's Cradle" by Kurt Vonnegut
*"The Bridge of San Luis Rey" by Thornton Wilder: A Study Guide **
Study Guide on "The Book Thief" by Markus Zusak

Study Guides available as e-books:
Study Guide on "Heart of Darkness" by Joseph Conrad
Study Guide on "The Mill on the Floss" by George Eliot
Study Guide on "Lord of the Flies" by William Golding
Study Guide on "Nineteen Eighty-Four" by George Orwell
Study Guide on "Henry IV Part 2" by William Shakespeare
Study Guide on "Julius Caesar" by William Shakespeare
Study Guide on "The Pearl" by John Steinbeck
Study Guide on "Slaughterhouse-Five" by Kurt Vonnegut

New titles are added regularly.

Teacher resources:

Ray also publishes many more study guides and other resources for classroom use on the 'Teachers Pay Teachers' website:
http://www.teacherspayteachers.com/Store/Raymond-Moore

Made in the USA
Monee, IL
16 March 2021